JIHADIST SAFE HAVENS: EFFORTS TO DETECT AND DETER TERRORIST TRAVEL

HEARING

BEFORE THE

SUBCOMMITTEE ON COUNTERTERRORISM AND INTELLIGENCE

OF THE

COMMITTEE ON HOMELAND SECURITY HOUSE OF REPRESENTATIVES

ONE HUNDRED THIRTEENTH CONGRESS

SECOND SESSION

JULY 24, 2014

Serial No. 113–80

Printed for the use of the Committee on Homeland Security

Available via the World Wide Web: http://www.gpo.gov/fdsys/

U.S. GOVERNMENT PUBLISHING OFFICE

91–932 PDF   WASHINGTON : 2015

For sale by the Superintendent of Documents, U.S. Government Publishing Office
Internet: bookstore.gpo.gov   Phone: toll free (866) 512–1800; DC area (202) 512–1800
Fax: (202) 512–2104   Mail: Stop IDCC, Washington, DC 20402–0001

COMMITTEE ON HOMELAND SECURITY

MICHAEL T. MCCAUL, Texas, *Chairman*

LAMAR SMITH, Texas
PETER T. KING, New York
MIKE ROGERS, Alabama
PAUL C. BROUN, Georgia
CANDICE S. MILLER, Michigan, *Vice Chair*
PATRICK MEEHAN, Pennsylvania
JEFF DUNCAN, South Carolina
TOM MARINO, Pennsylvania
JASON CHAFFETZ, Utah
STEVEN M. PALAZZO, Mississippi
LOU BARLETTA, Pennsylvania
RICHARD HUDSON, North Carolina
STEVE DAINES, Montana
SUSAN W. BROOKS, Indiana
SCOTT PERRY, Pennsylvania
MARK SANFORD, South Carolina
CURTIS CLAWSON, Florida

BENNIE G. THOMPSON, Mississippi
LORETTA SANCHEZ, California
SHEILA JACKSON LEE, Texas
YVETTE D. CLARKE, New York
BRIAN HIGGINS, New York
CEDRIC L. RICHMOND, Louisiana
WILLIAM R. KEATING, Massachusetts
RON BARBER, Arizona
DONDALD M. PAYNE, JR., New Jersey
BETO O'ROURKE, Texas
FILEMON VELA, Texas
ERIC SWALWELL, California
VACANCY
VACANCY

BRENDAN P. SHIELDS, *Staff Director*
JOAN O'HARA, *Acting Chief Counsel*
MICHAEL S. TWINCHEK, *Chief Clerk*
I. LANIER AVANT, *Minority Subcommittee Staff Director*

———

SUBCOMMITTEE ON COUNTERTERRORISM AND INTELLIGENCE

PETER T. KING, New York, *Chairman*

PAUL C. BROUN, Georgia
PATRICK MEEHAN, Pennsylvania, *Vice Chair*
JASON CHAFFETZ, Utah
CURTIS CLAWSON, Florida
MICHAEL T. MCCAUL, Texas *(ex officio)*

BRIAN HIGGINS, New York
LORETTA SANCHEZ, California
WILLIAM R. KEATING, Massachusetts
BENNIE G. THOMPSON, Mississippi *(ex officio)*

MANDY BOWERS, *Subcommittee Staff Director*
DENNIS TERRY, *Subcommittee Clerk*
HOPE GOINS, *Minority Subcommittee Staff Director*

(II)

CONTENTS

JIHADIST SAFE HAVENS: EFFORTS TO DETECT AND DETER TERRORIST TRAVEL

Thursday, July 24, 2014

U.S. HOUSE OF REPRESENTATIVES,
COMMITTEE ON HOMELAND SECURITY,
SUBCOMMITTEE ON COUNTERTERRORISM AND INTELLIGENCE,
Washington, DC.

The subcommittee met, pursuant to call, at 10:04 a.m., in Room 311, Cannon House Office Building, Hon. Peter T. King [Chairman of the subcommittee] presiding.

Present: Representatives King, Broun, Clawson, Higgins, and Thompson.

Mr. KING. Good morning. First of all, thank you for being here. It is really—it is very much appreciated. I know I speak for the Ranking Member, as well.

The Committee on Homeland Security, Subcommittee on Counterterrorism and Intelligence will come to order. The subcommittee is meeting today to hear testimony examining jihadist safe havens and efforts to detect and deter terrorist travel. I now recognize myself for an opening statement.

Today we know at least 100 Americans have traveled or attempted to travel to Syria for the purpose of joining an Islamist extremist group, either al-Nusra Front, the Islamic State of Iraq and al-Sham (ISIS), or another. We also know that several thousand individuals from European nations have flocked to Syria, and likely now Iraq, for the same purpose.

Fifteen months ago, this subcommittee held a hearing on the growing threat posed to the homeland from al-Qaeda, which focused on foreign fighters from around the world converging on the war zone in Syria. Since that time, from all accounts, the situation has dramatically worsened. The number of al-Qaeda-affiliated and jihadist groups has multiplied.

In May 2014, FBI Director Comey noted that the current Syrian conflict, "is an order of magnitude" worse than Afghanistan in the 1980s and 1990s. With stunning velocity, the group formerly known as al-Qaeda in Iraq has evolved into the Islamic State of Iraq and al-Sham, and established what it calls a caliphate that spans across portions of Iraq and Syria.

While core al-Qaeda leadership may have diminished capacity, in recent months, it has sought to rebuild as U.S. forces withdraw from Afghanistan, and al-Qaeda affiliates around the world are as strong as ever. ISIS has ruthlessly captured cities, killed indiscriminately, and mobilized thousands of foreign fighters to its

(1)

cause. It moves its men and arms at will into safe havens on both sides of the Iraqi-Syrian border.

At least one American has died as a suicide bomber after spending 2 months in a training camp operated by al-Nusra Front in Aleppo. Twenty-two-year-old Moner Mohammed Abusalha, who was born and raised in Florida and reportedly traveled to Syria in late 2013, blew himself up in an attack in Syria on May 25, 2014.

The threat is not limited to U.S. persons fighting and being radicalized overseas or constrained to battlefields in Syria and Iraq. On May 24, French jihadist and Syrian war veteran Mehdi Nemmouche attacked a Jewish museum in Brussels.

Compounding the threat is the potential for terror groups to coordinate and share expertise, as well as fighters. Last month, we all followed press reports that members of al-Nusra had possibly linked up with bomb-making experts from AQAP, al-Qaeda in the Arabian Peninsula. The potent combination of AQAP's bomb-making expertise and al-Nusra's large pool of radical converts, including U.S. and European passport-holders, poses a severe threat to the homeland.

These concerns recently caused the United States to require additional security measures to enhance screening of travelers and luggage on U.S.-bound flights. Attorney General Holder's comments that, "the Syrian conflict has turned that region into a cradle of violent extremism," are important. As he said, the world cannot let it become a training ground from which our nationals can return and launch attacks.

Unfortunately, as we have seen too often, words from key administration officials have not translated into plans and action. Political instability and American disengagement in the region has created the conditions allowing radical jihadism to regenerate and metastasize. It is essential that the White House articulates American interests in the region and elicits greater cooperation from European and foreign partners to identify and track individuals seeking to join extremist groups.

As the diaspora of fighters and ideology spreads, there will be long-term consequences and a direct threat to the United States and to the West. It is time for the administration and the Congress to implement a plan to safeguard the homeland before Westerners who have become further radicalized in these conflicts are sent home to carry out attacks.

I especially want to thank Dr. Simcox and Dr. Jones, who have previously testified before our committee. We also want to welcome Fred Kagan, who I had the opportunity of meeting, I guess, 7 or 8 years ago now when you were in the process of formulating the surge policy in Iraq, you and General Keane. I remember that meeting very well. And Peter Brookes, who has been a long-time warrior in this fight against terrorism.

So you are here to put ISIS's growth in perspective, a group which was not even discussed a year ago, but now controls large portions of territory in Syria and Iraq and poses a significant threat to the United States. I look forward to the panel's update and would like to thank our distinguished panel of witnesses in advance.

[The statement of Chairman King follows:]

STATEMENT OF CHAIRMAN PETER T. KING

Today we know that at least 100 Americans have traveled or attempted to travel to Syria for the purpose of joining an Islamist extremist group, either al-Nusrah Front, the Islamic State of Iraq and al-Sham (ISIS), or another. We also know that several thousand individuals from European nations have flocked to Syria, and likely now Iraq, for the same purpose.

Fifteen months ago, this subcommittee held a hearing on the growing threat posed to the homeland from al-Qaeda, which focused on foreign fighters from around the world converging on the war zone Syria. Since that time, from all accounts the situation has dramatically worsened. The number of al-Qaeda-affiliated and jihadist groups have multiplied. In May 2014, FBI Director Comey noted that the current Syrian conflict "is an order of magnitude" worse than Afghanistan in the 1980s and 1990s. And with stunning velocity, the group formerly known as al-Qaeda in Iraq has evolved into the Islamic State of Iraq and al-Sham, and established what it calls a caliphate that spans across portions of Iraq and Syria.

While core al-Qaeda leadership may have diminished capacity, in recent months they have sought to rebuild as U.S. forces withdraw from Afghanistan, and al-Qaeda affiliates around the world are as strong as ever. ISIS has ruthlessly captured cities, killed indiscriminately, and mobilized thousands of foreign fighters to its cause. It moves its men and arms at will into safe havens on both sides of the Iraqi-Syrian border.

At least one American has died as a suicide bomber after spending 2 months in a training camp operated by al-Nusrah Front in Aleppo. Twenty-two-year-old Moner Mohammed Abusalha, who was born and raised in Florida and reportedly traveled to Syria in late 2013, and blew himself up in an attack in Syria on May 25, 2014.

The threat is not limited to U.S. persons fighting and being radicalized overseas, or constrained to battlefields in Syria and Iraq. On May 24, French jihadist and Syrian war veteran Mehdi Nemmouche attacked a Jewish museum in Brussels.

Compounding the threat is the potential for terror groups to coordinate and share expertise, as well as fighters. Last month, we all followed press reports that members of al-Nusrah had possibly linked up with bomb-making experts from al-Qaeda in the Arabian Peninsula (AQAP). The potent combination of AQAP's bomb-making expertise and al-Nusrah's large pool of radical converts including U.S. and European passport holders, poses a significant threat to the homeland. These concerns recently caused the United States to require additional security measures at certain foreign airports to enhance screening of travelers and luggage on U.S.-bound flights.

Attorney General Eric Holder's comments that "the Syrian conflict has turned that region into a cradle of violent extremism," are important. As he said, "the world cannot let it become a training ground from which our nationals can return and launch attacks." Unfortunately, as we have seen far too often, words from key administration officials, including the President, have not translated into plans and action. Political instability and American disengagement in the region has created the conditions allowing radical jihadism to re-generate and metastasize.

It is essential that the White House articulates American interests in the region, and elicits greater cooperation from European and foreign partners to identify and track individuals seeking to join extremist groups. As the diaspora of fighters and ideology spreads, there will be long-term consequences and a direct threat to the United States and the West. It is time for the administration to implement a plan to safeguard the homeland before Westerners who have become further radicalized in these conflicts are sent home to carry out attacks.

I would like to welcome back Mr. Simcox and Dr. Jones, who testified at our hearing last year. It appears that over the last year the situation on the ground has gotten substantially worse for American interests in the region. To put ISIS's growth in perspective—a group not discussed a year ago now controls large portions of territory in Syria and Iraq and poses a significant threat to the United States.

I look forward to the panel's update, with the additional input from Dr. Kagan and Dr. Brookes, on the spreading conflict and would like to thank our distinguished panel of witnesses in advance.

Mr. KING. With that, I yield to the Ranking Member from New York, Mr. Higgins.

Mr. HIGGINS. Thank you, Chairman King, for holding this hearing. This hearing is a timely and necessary follow-up to our hearing last May regarding al-Qaeda operations in both Iran and Syria. I would also—I think that is supposed to be Iraq.

I would also like to thank the witnesses for appearing to testify as we expand our understanding about travel patterns of foreign fighters in Syria and Iraq and how they continue to impact the United States homeland. U.S. intelligence officials report that at least 7,000 fighters from more than 50 countries across the Middle East, North Africa, Europe, Asia, including dozens of volunteers from the United States, have traveled to Syria to support armed opposition groups there.

Other estimates by non-governmental sources suggested over 100,000 pro-opposition foreign fighters have traveled to Syria. Overall, the United States Government estimates place the strength of armed opposition forces, including foreign fighters, between 75,000 and 110,000 persons. Some of these opposition groups are U.S.-designated terrorist organizations, and a subset of dedicated extremist fighters may pose an outsized threat. Thousands of other non-Syrian fighters reportedly are fighting in Syria to support the government of Bashar al-Assad, including members of Lebanese Hezbollah, the Iranian military, and Iraq-Shia militias.

Foreign fighters contribute to the persistence of the armed conflict in Syria, and they also pose external security risks now or in the near future. To date, the FBI has arrested a handful of U.S. citizens and residents on charges of providing material support to terrorist groups and using certain weapons in connection with the conflict in Syria.

Officials in European and Asian governments have also made several arrests of would-be foreign fighters, returned foreign fighters or their recruiters and facilitators. It is imperative that the United States focus not only on the United States persons traveling to and from Syria, but also persons traveling to and from our neighboring countries, as well.

On April 22, 2013, the Canadian police announced the arrest of two people in connection with plotting a terrorist attack on a passenger train that travels from Toronto through Niagara Falls, New York, and into New York City. According to Canadian officials, the alleged terrorists were receiving assistance from al-Qaeda elements in Iran. Last year's plot in Canada raises questions both about whether al-Qaeda operatives in Iran and Syria have access to a broader terror network and whether Canada is a target for terrorist activity or recruitment.

Today, in addition to their testimony on the larger issues of foreign fighters, I would ask our witnesses to provide information on foreign fighters in Canada and the potential for these individuals to enter the United States via Canada after returning from Syria or Iraq.

Again, I look forward to today's testimony. With that, I will yield back.

[The statement of Ranking Member Higgins follows:]

STATEMENT OF RANKING MEMBER BRIAN HIGGINS

JULY 24, 2014

This hearing is a timely and necessary follow-up to our hearing last May regarding al-Qaeda operations in both Iran and Syria. I would also like to thank the witnesses for appearing to testify as we expand our understanding about travel patterns of foreign fighters in Syria and Iraq and how they continue to impact on the U.S. homeland.

U.S. intelligence officials report that at least 7,000 fighters from more than 50 countries across the Middle East, North Africa, Europe, Asia, including dozens of volunteers from the United States, have traveled to Syria to support armed opposition groups there. Other estimates by non-Government sources suggest that over 10,000 pro-opposition foreign fighters have travelled to Syria. Overall, U.S. Government estimates place the strength of armed opposition forces—including foreign fighters—between 75,000 and 110,000 persons.

Some of these opposition groups are U.S.-designated terrorist organizations, and a subset of dedicated extremist fighters may pose an outsized threat. Thousands of other non-Syrian fighters reportedly are fighting in Syria to support the government of Bashar al Assad, including members of Lebanese Hezbollah, the Iranian military, and Iraqi Shia militias.

Foreign fighters contribute to the persistence of the armed conflict in Syria and may also pose external security risks now or in the near future. To date, the FBI has arrested a handful of U.S. citizens and residents on charges of providing material support to terrorist groups and using certain weapons in connection with the conflict in Syria.

Officials in European and Asian governments have also made several arrests of would-be foreign fighters, returned foreign fighters, or their recruiters and facilitators. It is imperative that United States focus not only on U.S. persons traveling to and from Syria, but also persons traveling to and from our neighboring countries as well.

On April 22, 2013, the Canadian Police announced the arrest of two people in connection with plotting a terrorist attack on a passenger train that travels from Toronto, through Niagara Falls, New York, into New York City. According to Canadian officials, the alleged terrorists were receiving assistance from al-Qaeda elements in Iran.

Last year's plot in Canada raises questions both about whether al-Qaeda operatives in Iran and Syria have access to a broader terror network, and whether Canada is a target for terrorist activity or recruitment.

Today, in addition to their testimony on the larger issues of foreign fighters, I would like our witnesses to provide information on foreign fighter transit in Canada, and the potential for these individuals, to enter the United States via Canada after returning from Syria or Iraq.

Mr. KING. The gentleman yields back.

Other Members of the committee are reminded that opening statements may be submitted for the record.

[The statement of Ranking Member Thompson follows:]

STATEMENT OF RANKING MEMBER BENNIE G. THOMPSON

JULY 24, 2014

As the committee continues examine the homeland security implications of foreign fighting, it is important to revisit the facts that have lead us to this point. As fighting continues across Syria, government forces and their allies are being pitted against a range of anti-government insurgents. The disorder is so rampant that at times, many of these insurgent groups are even fighting amongst themselves.

While the total population of Syria is more than 22 million, the Civil War has driven more than 2.8 million Syrians into neighboring countries as refugees, since March 2011. Millions more Syrians are internally displaced and in need of humanitarian assistance, of which the United States remains the largest bilateral provider, with more than $2 billion in funding.

The United States also has allocated a total of $287 million to provide non-lethal assistance to select groups. While it is difficult to know exactly what is happening on the ground in Syria, as it changes day-to-day, it seems neither pro-Assad forces nor their opponents are capable of achieving outright victory in the short term.

In the interim, conflict between the Islamic State of Iraq and the Levant (ISIL) and other anti-Assad forces has also caused an increase in war fighting. Outside of Syria, the Syrian Civil War has caused an increase of religious-sect and political group conflicts in Iraq and Lebanon. It is clear that the Syrian conflict has national security implications that can be felt across the globe.

However, the current humanitarian and security crises within Syria are beyond the power of any single actor to resolve, including the United States. Top U.S. officials have made public statements warning that Syria-based extremists may pose a direct terrorist threat to the United States, including some foreign fighters who hold U.S., Canadian, or European passports.

Director of National Intelligence James Clapper has stated that an al-Qaeda-affiliated group within Syria "does have aspirations for attacks on the homeland."

Central Intelligence Agency Director, John Brennan, has publically identified al-Qaeda-tied groups and the Islamic State of Iraq and the Levant (ISIL) within Syria as a concern for the recruitment of individuals and the development of capabilities to be able to carry out attacks inside of Syria and also to use Syria as a launching pad.

In February of this year, as his first public address as Secretary, Department of Homeland Security Secretary Jeh Johnson acknowledged that Syria has become a matter of homeland security.

He did so because U.S. law-enforcement and intelligence officials know individuals from North America and Europe are heading to Syria and will be exposed to radical and extremist influences before possibly returning to their home countries with intent to do harm.

Amid all the human suffering, in-fighting, and homeland security implications, it may seem lost that the Syrian conflict was once a mass civic movement advocating for greater political freedom.

It is imperative for us to focus diplomatic efforts on coordinating with foreign fighter source, transit, and returnee destination countries to strengthen shared responses and preventive measures. I hope our conversation today provides insight into the full scope of the foreign fighter issues and how both U.S. and international officials can work to coordinate both intelligence and response efforts.

Mr. KING. We are—as I said before—pleased to have a very distinguished panel of witnesses before us today on this important topic.

Our first witness will be Dr. Fred Kagan, who is the Christopher DeMuth chair and director of the American Enterprise Institute's Critical Threats Project. This project is dedicated to tracking and analyzing key and emerging National security threats to our Nation in order to inform on-going policy discussions. Prior to joining AEI, Dr. Kagan was a professor of military history at West Point. As I mentioned before, my first dealing with Dr. Kagan was back in 2007 when he I thought presented the most cogent analysis—you and General Keane—of the situation in Iraq and really laid out a battle plan and message which did succeed. Unfortunately, that has not been followed-up on, but I want to thank you for your service and I look forward to your testimony.

Dr. Kagan, you are recognized.

STATEMENT OF FREDERICK W. KAGAN, DIRECTOR, CRITICAL THREATS PROJECT, AMERICAN ENTERPRISE INSTITUTE

Mr. KAGAN. Thank you, Mr. Chairman, and Ranking Member, and thanks to the committee for holding this hearing. One of the things that has struck me is that in the midst of a public policy debate that is sometimes not well-moored in reality, the discussions that I have had about these topics on the Hill have been very serious and very thoughtful and very bipartisan. I think that that is a testimony to the seriousness with which you all take the security of the United States, and I am grateful to you for it.

The establishment and expansion of the Islamic State in Iraq and Syria represents a step change in the threat to American homeland security and National security generally. This is the first time that an al-Qaeda-affiliated group has made the leap from stateless terrorist organization to a quasi-state with a combat-effective army and the resources of a modern urban region at its disposal.

The Islamic State has declared its intention of attacking Americans and is actively recruiting U.S. and European passport-holders. It has acquired radioactive material from Mosul University and many millions of dollars from banks in Mosul and Anbar. We have never seen an al-Qaeda threat of this magnitude before, and we must face it squarely now or face the consequences later.

The Islamic State's relationship with al-Qaeda and its leader, Ayman al-Zawahiri, is complex and fraught. The Islamic State evolved from the organization known as al-Qaeda in Iraq, which was a formal and recognized al-Qaeda affiliate. The group changed its name to the Islamic State of Iraq in 2006, and al-Qaeda leadership accepted that change, although grudgingly. When it began calling itself the Islamic State of Iraq and al-Sham, ISIS, in 2013, however, asserting its control over the operations of al-Qaeda affiliate Jabhat al-Nusra in Syria, Zawahiri balked. Jabhat al-Nusra protested vigorously and appealed to Zawahiri, who ruled on its behalf and ordered ISIS to confine itself to Iraq.

The ISIS leader, Abu Bakr al-Baghdadi, now styling himself as Caliph Ibrahim, rejected Zawahiri's order, leading to an escalating rhetorical fight that ended with Zawahiri expelling ISIS from al-Qaeda, at least the portion of ISIS that was in Syria in early 2014. It was never clear, however, that Zawahiri was denying the continued validity of the al-Qaeda franchise in Iraq. It is my assessment that ISIS, the Islamic State, that is, remains a part of the larger al-Qaeda family, whatever its formal affiliation with the group might be.

Other groups within the larger al-Qaeda-associated family have established statelets and armies before. The Afghan Taliban had both in the 1990s. Al-Shabaab had much more constrained versions in Somalia after 2009. Al-Qaeda in the Arabian Peninsula briefly ruled parts of Abyan and Shabwah provinces in Yemen, although its rule and its conventional military capabilities proved too tenuous to hold.

None of these situations were remotely as dangerous to the United States as the Islamic State is today, largely because they occurred in areas of the world that were impoverished, lacked basic resources, let alone the advanced technological, human capital, and financial resources of the areas they now control in Iraq and Syria.

Recognizing the danger is not the same as seeing a solution, however. The Islamic State was able to advance rapidly because hollowed-out and demoralized Iraqi security forces in the north collapsed. Its advance ceased for the moment in large part because of the mobilization of Iranian-backed Shia militias and an armed populace. Even so, Iran has had to deploy probably hundreds of members of its own IRGC, the commander of its Quds Force, Qassem Soleimani, and elements of the IRGC air force, as well, to stave off the Islamic State's attacks.

The situation remains tenuous, and the security of Baghdad is by no means as certain as many appear to believe. The Islamic State is not 10 feet tall, but neither is it negligible, and nor is its collapse inevitable.

The Iranian presence and obvious fear of the Islamic State has led some Americans to muse on the feasibility of either letting the Iranians fight this fight for us or even actively cooperating with

Tehran against a common enemy. This superficially plausible strategy will not survive contact with the reality that the Iranian leadership sees the Islamic State as an American-created and -supported tool for retaining U.S. influence in the region having abandoned Iraq and Afghanistan and lost in Syria.

Supreme Leader Ayatollah Ali Khamenei and his closest associates have categorically rejected cooperation with the United States in Iraq, even in the midst of the nuclear negotiations. Even if we could somehow persuade Khamenei to work with us, the results would not be satisfactory. It is, after all, Iranian policy and strategy that helped get us to this point. Iran consistently pursues a sectarian approach to the conflict that fuels the flames of the insurgency and creates fertile ground for recruitment for al-Qaeda.

The prospect of sending American ground forces back into Iraq is distasteful, to say the least. Some have argued for a sort of expanded drone campaign—expanded from nothing, by the way, because until the fall of Mosul, we were taking reportedly absolutely no actions against growing al-Qaeda franchises in Iraq and Syria, creating one of the largest safe havens for those two groups anywhere in the world.

But even an expanded drone campaign will fail. Even air strikes will fail. As Brett McGurk recently testified, we are now looking at a full-blown army with a state, not a terrorist organization. The track record of these kinds of attacks even against terrorist organizations is extremely limited.

We need to do a few things to address this problem right now, and then we need to think hard about what the long-term solutions are going to be. It starts, of course, with recognizing the magnitude of the threat. Of course, ISIS, or the Islamic State, is only part of that threat.

It starts with recognizing that we have to stop the process of disarming ourselves. We have to reverse the defense cuts that were made in the name of an austerity that seemed to have affected only the defense budget and that are out of touch with the reality of our time, when the tide of war is not receding, but rather flowing.

We also have to make the very unpalatable choice to recognize that we cannot continue to attack our intelligence community to strip it of its capabilities to watch growing threats and to provide warning in an era when the threats are growing and our capabilities for dealing with them have diminished.

I firmly believe in the principles of privacy and civil liberties and I believe that we must do everything in our power to defend those core principles of the American way of life, but we also need to recognize that nothing is more dangerous to that way of life and to our civil liberties over the long run than the prospect of renewed terrorist attacks that will drive fear and stampede us into eliminating all of those protections.

If we want to protect our way of life, we have to protect ourselves against attack now, and that means that we have to invest in and support our armed forces and our intelligence community, while simultaneously developing a very complicated and very difficult, probably expensive strategy for dealing with an extremely serious threat.

I thank the committee for its time.

[The prepared statement of Mr. Kagan follows:]

PREPARED STATEMENT OF FREDERICK W. KAGAN

JULY 24, 2014

The establishment and expansion of the Islamic State in Iraq and Syria (IS) represents a step-change in the threat to American homeland security and National security generally. This is the first time that an al-Qaeda-affiliated group has made the leap from stateless terrorist organization to a quasi-state with a combat-effective army and the resources of a modern urban region at its disposal. The Islamic State has declared its intention of attacking Americans and is actively recruiting U.S. and European passport holders. It has acquired radioactive material from Mosul University and many millions of dollars from banks in Mosul and Anbar. We have never seen an al-Qaeda threat of this magnitude before and we must face it squarely now—or face the consequences later.

The Islamic State's relationship with al-Qaeda and its leader, Ayman al-Zawahiri, is complex and fraught. The IS evolved from the organization known as al-Qaeda in Iraq, which was a formal and recognized al-Qaeda affiliate. The group changed its name to the Islamic State of Iraq in 2006, and al-Qaeda leadership accepted that change, although grudgingly. When it began calling itself the Islamic State of Iraq and al-Sham (ISIS) in 2013, however, asserting its control over the operations of al-Qaeda affiliate Jabhat al-Nusra in Syria, Zawahiri balked. Jabhat al-Nusra protested vigorously and appealed to Zawahiri, who ruled on its behalf and ordered ISIS to confine itself to Iraq. The ISIS leader, Abu Bakr al Baghdad (now styling himself as Caliph Ibrahim), rejected Zawahiri's order, leading to an escalating rhetorical fight that ended with Zawihiri expelling ISIS from al-Qaeda—at least, the portion of ISIS that was in Syria in early 2014. It was never clear that Zawahiri was denying the continued validity of the al-Qaeda franchise in Iraq.

This dispute led to commentary suggesting that ISIS was no longer part of al-Qaeda, which has led to a certain confusion in policy discussions. But the intra-al Qaeda tensions are actually of interest only to students of al-Qaeda and those who parse the 2001 Authorization to Use Military Force (AUMF) with a microscope. In reality, IS remains a part of the global al-Qaeda movement. It is pursuing the same ideology—the argument, in fact, was over the fact that Zawahiri thinks that Caliph Ibrahim is moving too fast along the path toward the global caliphate. It continues to draw on the same pool of financial supporters, recruiters, and would-be suicide bombers or transnational fighters. It remains, in other words, a serious threat to the United States and the West.

Other groups within the larger al-Qaeda-associated family have established statelets and armies before. The Afghan Taliban had both in the 1990s. Al-Shabaab had much more constrained versions in Somalia after 2009. Al-Qaeda in the Arabian Peninsula briefly ruled parts of Abyan and Shabwah Provinces in Yemen, although its rule and its conventional military capabilities proved too tenuous to hold. None of these situations were remotely as dangerous to the United States as the Islamic State is today.

The Afghan Taliban ruled Afghanistan, to be sure, a fact that has made fighting its insurgency more difficult. But it was not an al-Qaeda franchise and did not espouse or pursue goals beyond Afghanistan. The country it ruled, moreover, was a war-shattered, poverty-stricken land that offered little in the way of advanced resources, or even basic resources, for that matter. Al-Shabaab was an al-Qaeda affiliate (although a secret one until 2012), but it also ruled one of the poorest regions of the world and, at that, its rule was heavily contested. Iraq is an advanced, urban society with a highly literate and technically-educated population, vast natural resources, and excellent infrastructure, even after many years of war. And the Islamic State has already demonstrated that its aims transcend Iraq and even Syria. It has set its immediate sights on Jordan and Lebanon and threatened Iran and us. The danger is unprecedented.

Recognizing the danger is not the same as seeing a solution, however. The IS was able to advance rapidly because hollowed-out and demoralized Iraqi Security Forces (ISF) in the north collapsed. Its advance was halted in large part because of the mobilization of Iranian-backed Shi'a militias and an armed populace. Even so, Iran has had to deploy probably hundreds of members of its own Islamic Revolutionary Guards Corps (IRGC), the commander of its Quds Force, Qassem Soleimani, and elements of the IRGC Air Force as well to stave off the Islamic State's attacks. The situation remains tenuous and the security of Baghdad is by no means as certain as many appear to believe. The Islamic State is not 10 feet tall, but neither is it negligible.

The Iranian presence and obvious fear of the IS has led some Americans to muse on the feasibility of either letting the Iranians fight this fight for us or even actively cooperating with Tehran against a common enemy. This superficially plausible strategy will not survive contact with the reality that the Iranian leadership sees the IS as an American-created and—supported tool for retaining U.S. influence in the region having abandoned Iraq and Afghanistan and lost in Syria. Supreme Leader Ayatollah Ali Khamenei and his closest associates have categorically rejected cooperation with the United States in Iraq—even in the midst of the nuclear negotiations when friendly overtures might have been expected—and ceaselessly repeat the mantra that the United States is backing the Islamic State.

Even if we could somehow persuade Khamenei to work with us in Iraq, the results would not be satisfactory. Iranian rhetoric is pan-Islamic, but its tools and techniques are narrowly sectarian. Khamenei is now backing Iraqi Prime Minister Nuri al Maliki for a third term, despite the insistence of the United States and all but the most sectarian Iraqi actors that he step aside. The Shi'a militias that are Iran's primary action arm in Iran also conduct sectarian killings that fan the flames of Sunni resentment and are important elements of the Islamic State's recruitment efforts. Iranian involvement in Iraq will make the situation worse, not better, and rapidly.

The prospect of sending American ground forces back into Iraq is distasteful, to say the least. Some have argued for a sort-of expanded drone campaign (expanded from nothing, by the way, since the United States had not been targeting al-Qaeda in Iraq or Syria at all before the fall of Mosul) or direct air support to Iraqi forces instead. This approach will fail. To begin with, air campaigns alone have never done more than disrupt terrorist organizations. Even the extremely aggressive drone program that decimated al-Qaeda in Pakistan was unable to destroy the group. But the IS is not a terrorist organization anymore. It is a small state and it has a small army. Targeted strikes will have even less effect on it, and they are likely to backfire.

The Iraqi Security Forces (to say nothing of Bashar al Assad's Syrian troops) have become sectarian. Iraqi social media refers to them as "Jaish al Maliki," Maliki's army, simultaneously dismissing the notion that they are Iraqi forces and equating them with the Jaish al Mahdi, the sectarian and Iranian-backed Shi'a militia formed by Moqtada al Sadr. If the United States simply provides air support to the ISF we will be seen as taking Maliki's (and Iran's) side against the Sunni. It is far from clear, moreover, that the ISF could retake the territories it has lost even with U.S. air support and without U.S. support on the ground. The United States had an extremely hard time, we should remember, driving al-Qaeda in Iraq from Baghdad and Mosul with 150,000 troops on the ground. The Iraqis will find it harder, not easier, because the ISF is regarded with such suspicion by many Sunni.

We may well face a simple and extremely unpalatable choice: Send at least some U.S. ground forces back to Iraq or watch the consolidation of the first-ever effective al-Qaeda state and army. There is no guarantee at all that sending U.S. forces back would eliminate the threat. Neither is there any reason for confidence that an al-Qaeda state in Iraq and Syria will not launch a campaign against the U.S. homeland and interests abroad.

Some will no doubt argue that the wisest course is to tend our own garden and focus on our own defenses rather than trying to intervene in an insanely complicated struggle. The trouble is that we are rushing to dismantle our defenses and make ourselves more vulnerable to the threat even as it grows exponentially. We are in the process of gutting our military in the name of an austerity that has not affected the parts of the Government that actually account for the massive increases in U.S. spending projected over the coming years. And we are dismantling our intelligence apparatus in the name of protecting privacy and civil liberty.

The defense of American civil liberties, including privacy, is of paramount importance. It can never be ignored or simply pushed aside in the interests of expediency. It must be balanced, however, against the need to defend American lives and homes, which is the first responsibility of Government. We are not currently striking that balance properly. We have allowed highly colored and selective leaks to instill fear in our hearts about what our intelligence community is doing, while ignoring the very real external threats that community is actually focused on watching.

There is no easy solution to the dilemmas posed here and I will not offer any. But the mandate of this committee requires it to evaluate all of the threats objectively and unemotionally and come to considered conclusions about how to strike the right balance. That evaluation must proceed, however, from an accurate and clear-eyed assessment of the actual threat. That threat is large and growing while our ability to defend ourselves is shrinking. We must reverse both trends, lest we face attacks in the future that may well change our society fundamentally. We can start by restoring defense cuts and re-considering the rush to outlaw specific intelligence programs whose merits cannot be debated publicly. This committee should, in fact, take the lead in developing and proposing expansions in U.S. intelligence capabilities that are coherent with the protection of civil liberties and privacy that is so vital to our democracy.

The challenges we face are great, but we must avoid taking counsel of our fears—fears of the enemy, fears of an unchecked government, fears of overseas involvement, or simply fears of the complexity of the problem. There is no certainty in acting, but there is no safety in passivity. I thank the committee for the opportunity to consider these challenges at this important moment in history.

Mr. KING. Thank you, Dr. Kagan.

Robin Simcox is a research fellow at the Henry Jackson Society in London, a bipartisan British-based think tank. His work focuses on terrorism and national security, specifically al-Qaeda, al-Qaeda affiliates, and terrorism trends. Prior to joining the society, Mr. Simcox was a research fellow at the Center for Social Cohesion, a think tank studying extremism and terrorism in the United Kingdom. Mr. Simcox testified previously before the subcommittee on the same issue. I guess that was about 15 months ago.

I want to thank for returning and thank you for your testimony. You are recognized.

STATEMENT OF ROBIN SIMCOX, RESEARCH FELLOW, THE HENRY JACKSON SOCIETY

Mr. SIMCOX. Chairman King, Ranking Member Higgins, Members of the subcommittee, thank you for inviting me here today.

In recent years, the United States and its allies have faced threats emanating from terrorist safe havens in countries such as Afghanistan, Pakistan, and Yemen. The most recent areas of concern to have developed are in Iraq and Syria.

In the short term, the greatest danger to emerge from these safe havens is the Islamic State of Iraq and al-Sham, ISIS, and also Westerners returning to their homeland having fought in Iraq and Syria.

ISIS controls a stretch of territory the size of Jordan. It has acquired recruits, weapons, and finances to the extent there is now more of a terrorist army than a terrorist group. Over the last decade, ISIS and its precursor groups have targeted not just Iraq, but Jordan, Lebanon, and Syria. It has also threatened Turkey. ISIS has succeeded in establishing a base in the Levant from which to expand its influence throughout the region.

Iraq fatigue in Washington and in London is significant. There will be a temptation to dismiss this as sectarian bloodletting or a largely irrelevant civil war. This temptation absolutely has to be avoided.

The danger posed by ISIS is real, enduring, and not limited to the Middle East. It has gone largely unnoticed that it has also been connected to a series of attacks in Europe over the last decade. This includes a June 2007 attack against targets in the United Kingdom, a suicide bombing in Sweden in 2010, and most recently the May 2014 shootings at the Jewish Museum in Brussels. This is not a group obsessed with only local sectarian concerns.

ISIS is now likely to attract fresh recruits, including those from the West, to its safe havens in Iraq, where they can receive training. Earlier this year, Abu Bakr al-Baghdadi, the supposed new caliph in ISIS, warned the United States that "soon we will be in direct confrontation." I would suggest we take him at his word.

However, the threat the West faces from terrorism today is obviously multi-pronged. An area of great concern to intelligence agencies is not just the dangers posed by terrorist groups operating in Iraq and Syria, but those returning to the West having fought there. I will focus specifically on the British angle.

It is thought that between 400 to 500 Brits have traveled to fight in the Syrian conflict, a higher number than in Afghanistan or in Iraq. Those fighters who return to the United Kingdom will likely do so battle-hardened, well-trained, and exposed to extremist ideology.

Not every returning fighter is going to try and aspire to carry out attacks domestically. Yet according to Henry Jackson Society Research, almost half of those who had committed al-Qaeda-related offenses in the United States had received terrorist training abroad. In the United Kingdom, it was over a quarter.

The United Kingdom has taken a tough stance on Syria-related offenses. Already in the last 18 months, there have been 65 Syria-related terrorism arrests. The first successful conviction occurred in May 2014, and others have already followed. This is a welcome change. Previously, not a single individual who fought in any other jihadist conflict abroad had been convicted for doing so in a British court.

The U.K. government has also stepped up stripping dual-national fighters of their British citizenship. This power was used 20 times last year, a significant increase on previous years. However, the United Kingdom's approach is not only based on tough measures against those who have already traveled.

Channel, the home office's de-radicalization program, is one alternative. Over 500 terror suspects have already been placed through this scheme, and this number will only grow as the fallout from Syria and Iraq continues. The police have also launched a national campaign of those who are concerned about their relatives traveling abroad, encouraging them to seek help from the authorities if so, with a particular focus being placed on women in these families.

Another approach to consider is one that has been launched in Belgium, where authorities discovered that some of those who had joined the rebels in Syria were still receiving social security benefits. It subsequently stopped these payments. This could act as an effective deterrent. If an aspiring fighter knows that his departure would lead to his family being evicted, for example, that may cause him to reconsider his options.

The United Kingdom and the United States face a differing level of threats from returnee fighters. The United States has yet to see the numbers travel that the United Kingdom has, although this probably has just as much to do with geographical proximity as it does ideological intent, yet I believe the solutions to be broadly similar.

Prosecution of terrorism-related activity when possible, monitoring those deemed to be most dangerous by domestic security agencies, coordinating our de-radicalization efforts, potentially removing citizenship and social security benefits. Ultimately we need to show an unflinching determination to face down the multitude of threats to the Western homeland.

Thank you for listening, and I am happy to try and answer any questions you may have.

[The prepared statement of Mr. Simcox follows:]

PREPARED STATEMENT OF ROBIN SIMCOX

JULY 24, 2014

In recent years, the United States and its allies have faced threats emanating from terrorist safe havens in countries such as Afghanistan, Pakistan, and Yemen. The most recent areas of concern to have developed are in Iraq and Syria. In the short term, the greatest danger to emerge from these safe havens is the Islamic State of Iraq and al-Sham (ISIS, and formerly known as the Islamic State of Iraq, or ISI, and al-Qaeda in Iraq) and Westerners returning to their homeland having fought in Iraq and Syria. Formulating effective policies to counter this threat is now a priority for the United States and its allies.

ISIS

The danger ISIS poses to the West is becoming increasingly clear, highlighted by General David Petraeus, European Union counterterrorism coordinator Gilles de Kerchove, and British Prime Minister David Cameron in recent weeks.[1] These concerns are understandable. ISIS now controls a stretch of territory the size of Jordan and has declared an Islamic caliphate, acquiring recruits, weapons, and money to the extent that it is now more of a terrorist army than a terrorist group.

ISIS has succeeded in establishing a base in the Levant from which to expand its influence throughout the region. In a recently-released ISIS video, a British jihadist proclaimed that ISIS "understand no borders" and will fight "wherever our sheikh wants to send us." He specifically cites Iraq, Jordan, Lebanon, and Syria as targets.[2] All of these countries have been targeted on multiple occasions for terrorist attack by ISIS and its precursor organisations in the last decade.

Yet the danger posed by ISIS is not limited to the Middle East. ISIS and its precursor groups have also been connected to a series of attacks in Europe over the last decade.

- The perpetrators of a June 2007 attack against targets in London and Glasgow, Scotland—operations which consisted of a car bombing attack on Glasgow Airport and car bombs in London's West End—had the telephone numbers of ISI members on their cell phones. At the time, counterterrorism officials called the Glasgow and London attacks "the closest collaboration" between ISI and terrorists outside the Middle East to date.
- In 2010, a captured senior ISI operative admitted to Iraqi forces that ISI was preparing to carry out an attack in the West at the end of the year. Later that year, Taimour Abdulwahab al-Abdaly, an Iraqi-born militant who was thought to have trained with ISI in Mosul, carried out a suicide attack in Stockholm, Sweden. ISI praised this attack and in an audio message released after his death, al-Abdaly cited the Swedish artist Lars Vilks' insulting cartoons of Islam's Prophet Mohammed as a motivation for his act. ISI had previously offered $150,000 to anyone who "slaughtered" Vilks.
- In June 2013, the Iraqi defense ministry said it had arrested members of a cell in Baghdad that had been attempting to manufacture chemical weapons to smuggle into Canada, the United States, and Europe.
- In May 2014, Mehdi Nemmouche, a French citizen thought to have joined ISIS in Syria, shot and killed three people at the Jewish Museum in Brussels. His gun was wrapped in an ISIS flag.[3]

While it is not known whether ISIS and its precursor groups directed or merely inspired these plots, it certainly appears connected to them. Therefore, ISIS is not just a local threat. Over the last decade, it has carried out attacks in four Middle Eastern countries and been connected to three others in Europe; offered financial reward for the assassination of Europeans; and allegedly planned to smuggle chemical weapons into the West. This is not the behaviour of a group obsessed with local, sectarian concerns.

---

[1] "ISIS' Western Ambitions", *Foreign Affairs*, 30 June 2014, available at *http://www.foreignaffairs.com/articles/141611/robin-simcox/isis-western-ambitions*.
[2] Ibid.
[3] Ibid.

"Iraq fatigue" in Washington and London is significant. There is a temptation towards isolationism: To dismiss this as sectarian bloodletting or a complex civil war which has no relevance to international security. This temptation must be avoided. Following its recent successes, ISIS is now likely to attract fresh recruits—including those from the West—to its safe haven in Iraq, where they can receive training and attempt to carry out terrorist attacks against the Western homeland.

Earlier this year, Abu Bakr al-Baghdadi, the supposed new caliph, warned the United States that, "soon we'll be in direct confrontation" and to "watch out for us, for we are with you, watching".[4] This warning should not be dismissed lightly.

RETURNING FIGHTERS

However, the threat the West faces from terrorism today is multi-pronged. An area of great concern to intelligence agencies is that of the dangers posed by those returning from fighting jihad in Syria.

The geographical proximity of Turkey to Syria has made accessing this conflict zone from Europe easier than past jihadist fronts. One analysis has concluded that as many as 2,000 Europeans have travelled to fight in Syria.[5]

Focusing specifically on the British angle, it is thought that between 400–500 Brits have done so.[6] This is a higher number than with the jihads in Afghanistan or Iraq near the beginning of the century.[7] Charles Farr, Britain's top counterterrorism official, stated this year that Syria was "different from any other counterterrorism challenge that [the United Kingdom] have faced since 9/11—because of the number of terrorist groups now engaged in the fighting, their size and scale, the number of people from this country who are joining them, ease of travel, availability of weapons and the intensity of the conflict".[8]

Those fighters who return to the United Kingdom will likely do so battle-hardened, well-trained, and exposed to extremist ideology. Richard Walton, speaking at the time as the head of the London Metropolitan Police's counter-terrorism unit, has described an attack in the United Kingdom by a fighter returning from Syria as "almost inevitable".[9]

It is unlikely that every returning fighter is going to be a national security threat and aspire to carry out attacks domestically. Yet according to Henry Jackson Society research, almost half of those who had committed al-Qaeda-related offenses in the United States had received terrorist training. Almost 1 in 5 had combat experience abroad.[10] In the United Kingdom, over a quarter of those who committed Islamism-related offenses had received training abroad.[11]

To add to these security concerns, there have been recent reports that bomb-makers in Yemen are co-ordinating their efforts with terrorists in Syria in order to construct undetectable explosives targeting Western aviation. This led to a new round of security measures across airports targeting cell phones and other electronic devices. Attorney General Eric Holder recently stated these new threats were something he found "more frightening" than anything else he'd seen in his time in office yet.[12] This is quite an admission when considering some of al-Qaeda in the Arabian

---

[4] Ibid.

[5] "Up to 11,000 foreign fighters in Syria; steep rise among Western Europeans", International Centre for the Study of Radicalisation, 17 December 2013, available at *http://icsr.info/2013/12/icsr-insight-11000-foreign-fighters-syria-steep-rise-among-western-europeans/*.

[6] "Iraq and Ending Sexual Violence in Conflict", House of Commons, 16 June 2014, available at *http://www.publications.parliament.uk/pa/cm201415/cmhansrd/cm140616/debtext/140-6160001.htm#14061619000710*; "Counter-terror cop: 500 Brits fighting in Syria and Iraq", *ITV*, 21 June 2014, available at *http://www.itv.com/news/update/2014-06-21/counter-terror-cop-500-brits-fighting-in-syria-and-iraq/*.

[7] "Europeans are flocking to the war in Syria. What happens when they come home?", *Washington Post*, 29 January 2014, available at *http://www.washingtonpost.com/world/europe/europeans-are-flocking-to-the-war-in-syria-what-happens-when-they-come-home/2014/01/29/772f56d0-88f6-11e3-833c-33098f9e5267_story.html?hpid=z3*.

[8] "Syria extremism is unlike any threat UK has seen since 9/11, security chief warns", *Evening Standard*, 25 February 2014, available at *http://www.standard.co.uk/news/uk/exclusive-syria-extremism-is-unlike-any-threat-uk-has-seen-since-911-security-chief-warns-9151894.html*.

[9] "Anti-terrorism chief warns of British girls inspired by Jihad", *Evening Standard*, 23 January 2014, available at *http://www.standard.co.uk/news/crime/exclusive-antiterrorism-chief-warns-of-british-girls-inspired-by-jihad-9080110.html*.

[10] Robin Simcox & Emily Dyer, *Al-Qaeda in the United States: A Complete Analysis of Terrorism Offenses* (Henry Jackson Society, February 2013).

[11] Robin Simcox, Hannah Stuart, Houriya Ahmed & Douglas Murray, *Islamist Terrorism: The British Connections* (Henry Jackson Society, July 2011).

[12] "Latest Syria Threat 'More Frightening Than Anything' Else, Holder Says", *ABC News*, 13 July 2014, available at *http://abcnews.go.com/ThisWeek/latest-syria-threat-frightening-holder/story?id=24538221*.

Peninsula's aspirational and actual attempts to target the United States in recent years (including bombs concealed in operatives' underwear, in printer toner cartridges or even surgically implanted; ricin and cyanide plots; and poisoning Western water and food supplies).[13]

MEASURES TAKEN BY THE UNITED KINGDOM

Attorney General Holder also recently spoke about the need for European nations to take a more pre-emptive approach in preventing its citizens travelling to Iraq or Syria in the first place, including undercover investigations and prosecuting those for preparatory acts of terrorism. In the United States, the material support law—which covered almost a quarter of all charges used in al-Qaeda related offenses in the United States[14]—is a useful piece of legislation for this type of crime. However, similar legislation does not exist in all countries that suffer from a severe terrorist threat. For example, it took France until 2012 to bring in a new statute that made "criminal association with the intent to commit terrorist acts" prosecutable.[15]

The United Kingdom has taken a tough stance on Syria-related offences. In the last 18 months there have been 65 Syrian-related arrests in the United Kingdom.[16] Some of these cases—such as that of former Guantanamo Bay detainee Moazzam Begg, who has been charged with providing terrorist training in Syria and raised funds to aid terrorist causes there[17]—are now beginning to work their way through the British court system. The first conviction of a British citizen relating to Syria-related terrorism offences occurred in May 2014 and others have already followed.[18]

This is a welcome change. Beforehand, not a single individual who fought in Afghanistan, Iraq, or any other jihadist conflict had been charged for doing so in a British court. This was largely a problem of political will, as well as some shortcomings in legislation. Yet this government has shown more determination to start prosecuting such offenses.

The government has also stepped up stripping dual national fighters in Syria of their British citizenship. Under the British Nationality Act, the home secretary can deprive someone of their citizenship if it "is conducive to the public good" and it does not leave them stateless. This power was used 20 times last year, which is a significant increase on previous years. While this does not only apply to jihadists in Syria—for example, it has also been used against those fighting in Somalia—one former Foreign & Commonwealth official has said that it is an "open secret" that it is being applied to the conflict there.[19]

Another available option—although not one that has been used so far—is the use of Terrorism Prevention and Investigation Measures (TPIMs), which enable the government to place a series of restrictions on the movements of terror suspects they are unable to deport or prosecute. TPIM subjects are, for example, given a curfew, an electronic tag, restricted from meeting certain individuals and attending certain mosques. While these are not measures available to the United States, the need to detain those who are deemed a national security threat but who the state may not

[13] "Terror Attempt Seen as Man Tries to Ignite Device on Jet", *New York Times*, 25 December 2009, available at *http://www.nytimes.com/2009/12/26/us/26plane.html?_r=0*; "Cargo plane bomb plot: ink cartridge bomb 'timed to blow up over US'", *The Telegraph*, 10 November 2010, available at *http://www.telegraph.co.uk/news/uknews/terrorism-in-the-uk/8124226/Cargo-plane-bomb-plot-ink-cartridge-bomb-timed-to-blow-up-over-US.html*; "Al-Qaeda Yemen plane bomb plot foiled by 'insider'", *BBC News*, 8 May 2012, available at *http://www.bbc.co.uk/news/world-us-canada-17994493*; "Al Qaeda's Body Bombs: Al-Asiri's Next Threat", *Newsweek*, 14 May 2012, available at *http://www.newsweek.com/al-qaedas-body-bombs-al-asiris-next-threat-65057*; Daniel Klaidman, *Kill or Capture: The War on Terror and the Soul of the Obama Presidency* (HMH), p. 216.

[14] Simcox & Dyer, *Al-Qaeda in the United States* (Henry Jackson Society, 2013).

[15] "Attorney General Holder Urges International Effort to Confront Threat of Syrian Foreign Fighters", United States Department of Justice, 8 July 2014, available at *http://www.justice.gov/opa/pr/2014/July/14-ag-704.html*.

[16] "UK will feel fallout of war in Syria 'for years to come', warns top Met officer", *Guardian*, 22 June 2014, available at *http://www.theguardian.com/world/2014/jun/22/uk-syria-islamic-extremism-isis-muthana-cressida-dick*.

[17] "Ex-Guantanamo Bay detainee Moazzam Begg charged with terror offences", *The Telegraph*, 1 March 2014, available at *http://www.telegraph.co.uk/news/uknews/terrorism-in-the-uk/10669848/Ex-Guantanamo-Bay-detainee-Moazzam-Begg-charged-with-terror-offences.html*.

[18] "Syria conflict: First Briton convicted of terrorist offences", *BBC News*, 20 May 2014, available at *http://www.bbc.co.uk/news/uk-27488006*; "Two British men admit to linking up with extremist group in Syria", *Guardian*, 8 July 2014, available at *http://www.theguardian.com/world/2014/jul/08/two-british-men-admit-linking-extremist-group-syria*.

[19] "No way back for Britons who join the Syrian fight, says Theresa May", *Independent*, 23 December 2013, available at *http://www.independent.co.uk/news/uk/politics/exclusive-no-way-back-for-britons-who-join-the-syrian-fight-says-theresa-may-9021190.html*.

be able to prosecute is certainly a dilemma that it is familiar with (those detained at Guantanamo Bay being the perfect example).

However, the United Kingdom's approach is not only based on tough measures against those who have already travelled. If prosecution is not possible, then Channel—the Home Office's de-radicalisation programme—is a viable alternative. Over 500 terror suspects have already been placed through this scheme, and this number will only grow as the fallout from Syria continues.[20] The police have also launched a national campaign aimed at supporting the families—with a focus on women—of those who are concerned about their relatives travelling abroad, encouraging them to seek help from authorities if so.[21]

Another approach to consider is one that has been launched in Belgium and which could be considered by the West more broadly. Belgian authorities discovered that some of those who had joined the rebels in Syria were still receiving social security benefits and subsequently stopped these payments.[22] This could act as an effective deterrent. If an aspiring fighter knows that his departure would lead to his family being evicted, for example, that may cause him to reconsider his options.

THE ON-GOING THREAT

The exact amount of fighters that have already returned to the United Kingdom is unknown. One security official claimed the number could be as high as 250.[23] However, since there is ambiguity over the amount who have already travelled, there will inevitably be ambiguity over how many have returned. The former head of counterterrorism at MI–6 has said it is "out of the question" to be able to monitor all those who have returned from fighting in Syria.[24] The United Kingdom simply does not have the capacity.

For example, in 2007, MI–5 acknowledged they were currently tracking 2,000 terror suspects in the United Kingdom.[25] Assuming that the threat has remained reasonably consistent—a safe assumption, considering that Britain has either suffered from, or managed to foil, at least one major terrorist plot approximately every year since 9/11 [26]—and assuming that 500 Brits have travelled to Syria, that would mean that Syrian returnees could take up a quarter of MI–5's casework.

In reality, the number will not be that high yet—some fighters have already been killed in Syria; others have no intention of ever returning; some will be legally barred from returning by the government; while others may not assessed to be a threat to the United Kingdom. Yet this gives some indication of the scale of work that Syrian returnees could cause British security agencies.

Furthermore, by its own admission MI–5 can only "hit the crocodiles nearest the boat" and has to "prioritise ruthlessly".[27] This means that someone who is on the periphery of the Security Services' radar eventually drops off. Inevitably, the wrong decisions are occasionally made. Last year, Michael Adebolajo, an extremist of interest to MI–5 who had previously attempted to travel to Somalia but not regarded as posing an imminent danger, stabbed a British soldier to death in broad daylight on the streets of London.

SHARED CHALLENGE

The United Kingdom and the United States face a differing level of threat from returnee fighters. The United States is yet to see the numbers travel to Syria that the United Kingdom has, although this probably has just as much to do with the

---

[20] "500 terror suspects 'deradicalised' by Home Office", *BBC News*, 26 March 2013, available at http://www.bbc.co.uk/news/uk-21940899.

[21] "Police make Syria plea to UK Muslim women", *BBC News*, 24 April 2014, available at *http://www.bbc.co.uk/news/uk-27131707.*

[22] "Belgian jihadists in Syria stripped of welfare benefits", *France 24*, 19 August 2013, available at *http://www.france24.com/en/20130819-belgian-jihadists-syria-stripped-welfare-payments-assad-antwerp/.*

[23] "After fighting in Syria 250 British jihadis are 'back in the UK' say intelligence officers", *Daily Mirror*, 21 June 2014, available at *http://www.mirror.co.uk/news/world-news/after-fighting-syria-250-british-3739504.*

[24] "'Not possible' to monitor all UK Syria fighters", *BBC News*, 23 June 2014, available at *http://www.bbc.co.uk/news/uk-27968963.*

[25] "'Thousands' pose UK terror threat", *BBC News*, 5 November 2007, available at *http://news.bbc.co.uk/1/hi/uk/7078712.stm.*

[26] Simcox, Stuart, Ahmed & Murray, *Islamist Terrorism* (Henry Jackson Society, 2011).

[27] "Could 7/7 Have Been Prevented? Review of the Intelligence on the London Terrorist Attacks on 7 July 2005", Intelligence & Security Committee, HM Government, May 2009, available at *https://www.gov.uk/government/uploads/system/uploads/attachment_data/file/224542/7-7_attacks_intelligence.pdf.*

geographical proximity as it does ideological intent. Despite this, the solutions are broadly similar.

Those who have attempted or successfully joined up with, fundraised for, and/or received training from terrorist groups in Iraq and Syria should be prosecuted. If prosecution is not possible, trained fighters assessed to be the most dangerous should be monitored by domestic security agencies. The United Kingdom can call upon Channel, its de-radicalization programme; in the United States, the Countering Violent Extremism initiative is a work in progress and our governments should continue to co-ordinate their efforts on this work. The removal of citizenship and social security benefits are other potentially useful National security tools.

Ultimately, we need to show an unflinching determination to face down the threats being posed to the West by the dangers emerging from this region.

Mr. KING. Thank you very much, Mr. Simcox.

Dr. Peter Brookes is a senior fellow at the Davis Institute for National Security and Foreign Policy at the Heritage Foundation. He is serving his fourth term as a Congressionally-appointed member of the U.S.-China Economic and Security Review Commission and previously served in the President George W. Bush administration as deputy assistant secretary for defense for Asian and Pacific affairs and has been commenting on these issues as far as I can recall ever since al-Qaeda really emerged on the world scene.

So, Dr. Brookes, it is really a privilege to have you here today.

STATEMENT OF PETER BROOKES, SENIOR FELLOW, NATIONAL SECURITY AFFAIRS, DAVIS INSTITUTE FOR NATIONAL SECURITY AND FOREIGN POLICY, THE HERITAGE FOUNDATION

Mr. BROOKES. Thank you. Thank you very much. Thank you, Mr. Chairman, Members of the committee. Thank you for the opportunity to share my views today. I want to commend you, the committee and your staff, for highlighting this issue in this public setting. It comes none too soon, in my opinion. Of course, today the views I express today are my own.

I want to make three fundamental points. It is my view that Islamist militancy is on the march. I believe that we are facing increasing threats to the homeland as a result. I have concerns about current U.S. policy for dealing with it.

I never would have thought that 13 years after the 9/11 tragedy that we would still being dealing with the threat of Islamist terrorism, especially that associated with al-Qaeda, at such an elevated level. The al-Qaeda threat has proliferated significantly in recent years in my judgment.

Syria is a good example, as others have already mentioned, and should be of significant concern, considering the estimated number of violent jihadists that have gathered there to oppose the Bashar Assad regime. Iraq is also deeply afflicted with terrorism, especially the resurgence of al-Qaeda in Iraq off-shoots.

Of course, perhaps the most troubling development is the rise of the Islamic State in Syria and Iraq, ISIS, which has been capturing and perhaps holding a swath of significant territory that spans both Iraq and Syria. Elsewhere in the Middle East, al-Qaeda in the Arabian Peninsula may be the most dangerous al-Qaeda affiliate today. In South Asia, the Taliban and Haqqani Network violence is up in Afghanistan as the number of U.S. and foreign forces, the coalition forces, draws down.

In Africa, terrorists and violent extremists are thriving, as well. In Libya, the situation remains chaotic 3 years after the U.S.-

NATO-led operation. Of course, Libya was the location of the deadly September 11, 2012, attack on our diplomatic facilities in Benghazi. Algeria is afflicted by al-Qaeda in the Islamic Maghreb. AQIM is also active in nearby Mali, where violence is on the upswing after a French intervention slowed the terror group's advance.

Fighting with Boko Haram, Islamist militants in Nigeria, has resulted in a reported death of some 2,000 people just this year, the tragic kidnapping of hundreds of schoolgirls aside. In Somalia and Kenya, al-Shabaab—noted for its brazen Westgate Mall attack in 2013—is also gaining ground. In general, lawless, ungoverned, and/or chaotic places remain a significant counterterrorism problem.

What does this militant Islamist movement mean? In my opinion, it signifies that we are facing an increasing threat not only to U.S. interests overseas, but to the homeland. While not all of these al-Qaeda groups are directly targeting the U.S. homeland security currently, we should not embrace the notion that this view will not change in the future. Their objectives will not necessarily remain local or regional.

We should not assume that any seemingly overseas al-Qaeda threat will stay that way and will not evolve into a direct threat to the U.S. homeland. Indeed, intent can change quickly and may not be discovered by intelligence before it is too late.

While each terror group is unique, hostility towards the United States in my view is a common characteristic. While I understand and appreciate the hard work being done by intelligence, law enforcement, the military, and others in battling violent extremists and protecting the American homeland, I have concerns about current U.S. policy.

First, the rhetoric used by the Obama administration I believe has been misleading. Over time, the White House, including the President, has characterized al-Qaeda as on the run, on its heels, and decimated, and so forth.

Second, I am also troubled by other National security decisions. For instance, I believe the decision to withdraw from Iraq without provision of follow-on forces directly contributed to, along with other factors, the dire situation that exists there today. I believe that the security vacuum that will be left by the drawdown of U.S. forces in Afghanistan in the coming years, which could result in a total withdrawal, could be filled by al-Qaeda-affiliated groups over time as happened in Iraq.

Third, from a practical standpoint, I believe that the reluctance to influence or follow through on events in the Middle East/North Africa, such as Libya and the Arab Spring, especially the events in Syria, have not served our National interests well. Indeed, while a direct cause and effect is difficult to prove, I would suggest that a case could be made which claims that the failure of U.S. policies in Iraq and Syria had a hand in the success of ISIS today, which now stands as a significant National security threat.

Fourth, I am concerned that much of the world sees the United States in absolute—or at least relative—decline. I also believe that perception of American inattention, disinterest, or weakness in world affairs will drive policies and actions directed towards us, including provocations from militant Islamist extremists.

Fifth, I am also worried that U.S. counterterrorism policy is meant more to contain than eliminate al-Qaeda threats. Relying too heavily on the political will of foreign governments and the capabilities of other nations' counterterror forces or militaries to battle terror groups may be a losing, indeed, dangerous, proposition or strategy.

In conclusion, I would assert that parts of the world are aflame with Islamist militancy and that we are in the crosshairs. We have already weathered some 60 terrorist plots and/or attacks since 9/11, according to Heritage Foundation data. This is clearly no time for contentment with the status quo.

The concern is that some believe we are in a post-Osama bin Laden era. That is factually correct. But we are not in a post-terrorism or post-al-Qaeda period in my judgment. Osama bin Laden's and al-Qaeda's inspirational Islamist ideology of political violence lives on. Letting down our guard at this time in the face of this growing Islamist extremist reality would be a huge mistake and a major threat to our security and interests both at home and abroad.

Thank you very much.

[The prepared statement of Mr. Brookes follows:]

PREPARED STATEMENT OF PETER BROOKES

JULY 24, 2014

Mr. Chairman and Members of the committee: Thank you for this opportunity to share my views on the subject of today's hearing. I want to commend you, the committee, and your staff for highlighting this issue in this public setting. In my view, it comes none too soon.

Before I begin my testimony, let me say that the views I express today are my own and should not be construed as representing the official position of any of the organizations with which I am associated.

On the topic of today's hearing, I would like to make three fundamental points.

Quite simply, it is my view that Islamist militancy is on the march. Second, I believe we are facing increasing threats to the homeland as a result. And third, I have concerns about current U.S. policy for dealing with it.

Let me briefly expand on these points.

ISLAMIST MILITANCY IS ON THE MOVE

I never would have thought that nearly 13 years after the 9/11 tragedy that we would still being dealing with the threat of Islamist terrorism, especially that associated with al-Qaeda, at such an elevated level.

The al-Qaeda threat, whether by groups that have a direct association with al-Qaeda's core, exist as an off-shoot, or merely embrace its ideology, has proliferated significantly in recent years in my judgment.

The increasing diversity and the intensity of the Islamist terrorist threat, in my mind, means we have to defend against a growing number of different threat vectors, making it more difficult for our intelligence, law enforcement, and military efforts to succeed, whether at home or overseas.

We are all painfully aware of the rise of violent extremists across the globe. Indeed, the State Department reports that terrorist attacks were up more than 40 percent last year.

Syria is a good example, and should be of significant concern, considering the estimated number of violent jihadists that have gathered there to oppose the Bashar Assad regime.

As the committee knows, an estimated 7,000–12,000 foreign fighters from some 70–80 countries have reportedly gathered in Syria, perhaps constituting what experts believe is the largest contingent of violent extremists in any one place at any one time, including in pre-9/11 Afghanistan.

Iraq is also deeply afflicted with terrorism, especially the resurgence of al-Qaeda in Iraq off-shoots, which seemed to have been almost extinguished by the end of the U.S. surge in Iraq. Last year, Iraq suffered some 5,000–9,000 casualties as a result of terrorist and sectarian violence, according to various sources.

Of course, perhaps, the most troubling development is the rise of the Islamic State in Syria and Iraq (ISIS) which has set about capturing—and perhaps holding—a swath of significant territory that spans both Iraq and Syria.

Within this territory, ISIS has declared a caliphate, which not only threatens the regimes in Baghdad and Damascus, but which may prove over time to be a safe haven for terrorist planning, training, and operations beyond Iraq and Syria.

This newest caliphate is likely to resonate with Islamists on a number of levels around the globe. The allure of a new Islamist state may lead to more recruits, funding, and alliances. Moreover, ISIS' early success may encourage others to undertake the same thing elsewhere.

Indeed, even prior to the establishment of the "Islamic State," there were reports of the development of camps for not only training fighters for opposing the Syrian and Iraqi regimes, but for training foreign fighters to return to their native lands, especially Europe and the United States, to undertake terror attacks there.

Of course, the problem is not limited to Iraq and Syria.

Elsewhere in the Middle East, al-Qaeda in the Arabian Peninsula (AQAP), which is resident in Yemen, may be the most dangerous al-Qaeda affiliate today. It has held territory in Southern Yemen and its bomb-making prowess is well-known based on a number of spectacular plots by its innovative explosives expert, Ibrahim al Asiri.

In South Asia, Taliban and Haqqani Network violence is up in Afghanistan as the number of U.S. and foreign forces draws down, according to news outlets. These terror groups have historically found safe haven in neighboring Pakistan, which has severely impacted U.S. and Coalition counterinsurgency and terror operations in Afghanistan.

In Africa, terrorists and violent extremists are thriving as well. In Libya, the situation remains chaotic 3 years after the U.S.-NATO operation led to the demise of Libyan strongman Moammar Qaddafi. Libyan militias, including al-Qaeda-associated groups like Ansar al Sharia, continue to threaten any semblance of stability.

Of course, Libya was the location of the deadly September 11, 2012 attack on our diplomatic facilities in Benghazi.

Algeria is afflicted by al-Qaeda in the Islamic Maghreb (AQIM); it has been linked to recent plots in France on the Eiffel Tower, Louvre, and a nuclear power plant, according to news accounts.

AQIM is also active in nearby Mali, where violence is on the up-swing after a French intervention slowed the terror group's advance. Moreover, press reports indicate that al-Qaeda-linked militants in Mali may be working with Nigeria's Boko Haram, a terror group causing increasing alarm.

News accounts indicate that fighting with Boko Haram Islamist militants in Nigeria has resulted in the death of some 2,000 people this year, the tragic kidnapping of hundreds of school girls aside. It also reportedly operates in Cameroon and Niger.

Across the continent in Somalia and Kenya, al-Shabab—noted for its brazen Westgate Mall attack in 2013—is gaining ground. The terror group also seems to be a significant draw for prospective militants from the United States, according to some research.

Indeed, some analysts believed that al-Shabab may have drawn or recruited more Americans than any other terror group, but it has now likely been outpaced by a surge to Syria and Iraq. Moreover, some assert al-Shabab is cooperating and coordinating with Boko Haram, further expanding the terror network on the continent.

In general, lawless, ungoverned, and or chaotic places remain a significant counterterrorism problem.

INCREASING THREATS TO THE HOMELAND

What does this militant Islamist movement mean? In my opinion, it signifies that we are facing an increasing threat not only to U.S. interests overseas, but to the homeland.

I do not have to tell the committee about the reports of nearly a hundred Americans and as many as 3,000 Europeans that have traveled to Syria—and perhaps now Iraq—to fight in the Syrian (and perhaps now Iraqi) civil war(s).

We must assume that based on open-source reporting that some of these Americans and Europeans will be recruited and trained in the terrorist dark arts while in Iraq and Syria with the intention of returning to their native countries to commit terror, if reports are accurate.

Recent violence and plots in places like Britain, Belgium, and Spain that are related to Syria means that the threat is not a prospective one, but one that is here and now.

Specifically, the recent reports of a possible terror plot involving explosive cell phones and or electronic devices that might be targeting U.S.-bound airliners out of Europe is of great concern—and may arguably represent the most imminent terror threat to the U.S. homeland today.

Even more troubling are the reports that this plot involved a synergistic effort between al-Qaeda operatives in Syria/Iraq and AQAP bomb-makers. This sort of transnational terrorist teamwork is very disconcerting.

But we should not be surprised.

Al-Qaeda, including Osama bin Laden, has long valued zealous religious converts, recruiting operatives in place, including via the internet, and travelers with passports that may be in or enter a target country with limited scrutiny to perform terrorist acts.

While not all of these al-Qaeda groups are directly targeting the U.S. homeland currently, we should not embrace the notion that this view will not change in the future; their objectives will not necessarily remain local or regional.

In my view, these terror groups, whose goals may seem local or regional at this time, may have fundamental needs that might need to be satisfied first (e.g., holding territory for planning, training, and operating; securing funding; and finding recruits) before looking at expanding their operations afield such as toward the United States.

Furthermore, from a strategic perspective, these terror groups may not want to encourage or give reason for opposition from the United States at this time.

The point here being is that we should not assume that any seemingly overseas al-Qaeda threat will stay that way and not evolve into a direct threat to the U.S. homeland. Indeed, intent can change quickly and may not be discovered by intelligence before it is too late.

While each terror group is unique, hostility toward the United States is a common characteristic, in my opinion.

U.S. POLICY CONCERNS

While I understand and appreciate the hard work being done by intelligence, law enforcement, the military, and others in battling violent extremists and protecting the American homeland, I have concerns about current U.S. policy.

First, the rhetoric used by the Obama administration has been misleading, in my view. Over time, the White House, including the President, has characterized al-Qaeda as "on the run," "on its heels," and "decimated," and so forth.

Suggesting such, especially as concerns al-Qaeda writ large, is unfortunately disingenuous. While the White House occasionally specified that it was referring to "al-Qaeda core" (essentially the perpetrators of the 9/11 attacks in Pakistan and Afghanistan) when it spoke of the terror group's supposedly diminished status, that was not always the case.

Indeed, I would suggest that the White House was attempting to create a narrative on its handling of National security, specifically al-Qaeda, that was arguably overly optimistic. Worse, it may have given the American public—and others—the impression that al-Qaeda was in its last throes.

The take down of Osama bin Laden supported that narrative.

The problem is that, yes, Osama bin Laden was dead, but al-Qaeda was still very much alive. I do not believe that this reality was conveyed accurately or adequately to the American people by the administration when it should have been part of our National security dialogue and debate.

I believe that the early, public Benghazi attack assessments, such as references to a provocative video, were also driven by the White House's chosen, perhaps politically-driven, National security narrative.

Second, I am also troubled by other National security decisions. For instance, I believe the decision to withdraw from Iraq without the provision of follow-on forces directly contributed to, along with other factors, the dire situation that exists there today.

In addition, I believe that the security vacuum that will be left by the drawdown of U.S. forces in Afghanistan in the coming years, which could result in a total withdrawal, could be filled by al-Qaeda-affiliated groups over time as happened in Iraq.

Third, from a practical standpoint, I believe that a reluctance to influence or follow through on events in the Middle East/North Africa such as Libya and the Arab Spring, especially the events in Syria, has not served our National interests well.

Indeed, while a direct cause and effect is difficult to prove, I would suggest that a case could be made which claims that the failure of U.S. policies in Iraq and Syria had a hand in the success of ISIS today which now stands as a significant National security threat.

Fourth, I am concerned that much of the world sees the United States in absolute—or at least relative—decline. I also believe that perceptions of American inattention, disinterest, or weakness in world affairs will drive policies and actions directed toward us, including provocations from militant Islamist extremists.

Fifth, I am also worried that U.S. counterterrorism policy is meant more to contain than eliminate al-Qaeda threats. In other words, we are containing threats in places like Syria/Iraq or Yemen, but not acting vigorously enough, or at all, to eliminate them.

Relying too heavily on the political will of foreign governments and the capabilities of other nations' counterterror forces or militaries to battle terror groups may be a losing, indeed dangerous, strategy whether it is Iraq, Afghanistan, or Yemen.

Specifically, I believe that we are facing increasing threats to our interests overseas and to the homeland as a result of our failure to develop effective counterterror policies, which have provided space for terrorists to plan, train, and operate.

CONCLUSION

I would assert that parts of the world are aflame with Islamist militancy—and that we are in the crosshairs. Wishing away the terrorist threat we face at home or abroad will not make it disappear. Indeed, worse, we are at risk of creating complacency at home and abroad about this growing threat.

Complacency about such a challenge can be a killer. We have already weathered some 60 terrorist plots and or attacks since 9/11, according to Heritage Foundation data. This is clearly no time for contentment with the status quo.

The concern is that some believe we are in a post-Osama bin Laden era. That is factually correct, but we are not in a post-terrorism or post-al-Qaeda period in my judgment. Osama bin Laden's and al-Qaeda's inspirational Islamist ideology of political violence lives on in Syria, Iraq, Yemen, Nigeria, Libya, Afghanistan, and elsewhere.

Letting our guard down to this growing Islamist extremist reality would be a huge mistake—and a major threat to our security and interests both at home and abroad.

Mr. KING. Thank you, Dr. Brookes.

Dr. Seth Jones, who is the director of International Security and Defense Policy Center at the Rand Corporation, as well as an adjunct professor at Johns Hopkins University School for Advanced International Studies. Previously, Dr. Jones served as the representative for the U.S. commander, U.S. Special Ops Command, to the assistant secretary of defense of special operations. Prior to that position, he served as a plans officer and adviser to the commanding general, U.S. special operations forces in Afghanistan, and specializes in counterinsurgency and counterterrorism, including a focus on Afghanistan, Pakistan, and al-Qaeda.

In a time of heightened partisanship in Washington, interesting to note that you have appeared as a Republican witness and today as a Democratic witness before this committee, which says a lot about you and your perspective, and also hopefully something about this committee and the fact that we do try to deal in a bipartisan way. I think the fact that you have been called by both parties as "their witness," says—you know, speaks volumes about your knowledge and your ability.

So, Dr. Jones.

STATEMENT OF SETH G. JONES, DIRECTOR, INTERNATIONAL SECURITY AND DEFENSE POLICY CENTER, THE RAND CORPORATION

Mr. JONES. Thank you very much, Chairman King, Ranking Member Higgins, other Members of the subcommittee, thanks for inviting us to testify on I think what is a very important subject at a very important time. I have divided my comments into four sections, as you will see build on each other.

The first is to emphasize what Chairman King and Ranking Member Higgins noted in their opening statements, which is that the United States does face a—what I consider a growing threat from violent extremists traveling to and returning from Syria and other locations. According to my own estimates, the number of Americans is now above 100, somewhere around 125, 130 Americans that have traveled or attempted to travel to Syria to assist rebel organizations.

I do think it is important to look at the data here that there appear to be a wide range of motivations. Some appear to be interested in conducting violent jihad with al-Qaeda organizations or jihadist organizations like ISIS. Some appear to be interested in primarily fighting Shia. Some appear to be interested in supporting Syrian—what you might call Syrian nationalist groups against the Assad regime, others providing humanitarian assistance. So identifying the purpose of the individual traveling is obviously important.

The numbers in Europe, as we heard from Mr. Simcox, are order of magnitude larger. I will come back to that issue in a moment. But as many as 2,500 potentially Sunni extremists from Europe have arrived in Syria between January 2012 and July 2014. I would note also that we have seen fairly large numbers, in the hundreds, also return from Syria into Europe.

Just to put this into perspective, according to data I have, Syria today has the largest numbers of Westerners in any jihadist battlefield in the modern era, larger in terms of Westerners than what we saw in Afghanistan during the 1980s against the Soviet Union, larger after the 2001 overthrow of the Taliban regime, larger than in Iraq, including after the 2000 U.S. invasion, Somalia, Yemen, Libya. So I think it is important in that sense to put this into perspective and why we should focus on the subject.

Second, the broader trends I think are important. According to a Rand report I recently authored and was published a few weeks ago, the trends here are a bit concerning. There has been a—according to our estimates—55 percent increase in the number of jihadist groups between 2010 and 2013. The largest number of that—percentage of that increase is in North Africa and in the Syria area.

In addition, the number of jihadists themselves, not groups but fighters, has roughly doubled during that same time period, with the largest numbers of fighters operating in the Syria and broader Levant area. So this does appear to be a growing problem, and we can talk about the reasons for that in the discussion afterwards.

As Dr. Brookes noted earlier, not all of these groups present a direct threat to the U.S. homeland. Nusra and ISIS and some of the groups operating in Syria and Iraq appear to be primarily focusing on targets inside of Syria and inside of Iraq, but I would say that the trends are concerning. The pipeline between Iraq and Europe, as well as other places, the United States, Australia, is growing, financing, recruitment, and potentially operatives, and there is always this—a concern about inspired individuals, not directly connected with these groups, but that have trained. So this trend is concerning.

Let me conclude, then, the fourth area which is detecting and deterring travelers. I just want to say, I appreciate the efforts of U.S. intelligence, law enforcement, military, diplomatic efforts to focus on this problem.

But let me highlight three issues worth considering. I have got a much longer list, but just want to highlight three for note here. One is—and this really is a European issue—again, the largest numbers of extremists that we have seen where there is a visa waiver potential are in Europe.

Criminalizing attendance, not just training, but attendance at terrorist training camps overseas I would assess would likely deter or could deter some terrorists from traveling. The United Kingdom appears to be the only or one of the only European Union countries with such a law. The United States prohibits attendance at terrorist camps overseas and will prosecute. I think encouraging the European countries to criminalize attendance, not just training, would be quite helpful.

Second issue is preemptive action. Norway, Netherlands, France are among the few European countries of the United Kingdom that have preemptively arrested extremists preparing to travel to Syria. That is before they go, but many do not—do not have laws on the books along those lines, so I think working with our European allies on ways to prevent them from leaving, if there is enough evidence, would be helpful. Again, some European countries have now passed laws.

The last thing I will just mention is we have got to find ways, I think, to fix loopholes in our system. The fact that apparently Abu-Salah was able to travel to Syria, return to the United States without our awareness, and then go back and blow himself up in Syria does raise questions about whether we missed this.

So let me conclude by saying, I think this issue is very important. Thank you for calling this hearing. I look forward to the questions.

[The prepared statement of Mr. Jones follows:]

PREPARED STATEMENT OF SETH G. JONES [1][2]

JULY 24, 2014

Chairman King, Ranking Member Higgins, and Members of the subcommittee, thank you for inviting me to testify at this hearing, "Jihadist Safe Havens: Efforts to Detect and Deter Terrorist Travel."

My argument today is straightforward: The United States faces a threat from violent extremists, including Americans and other Westerners, in safe havens in Syria and other locations. Syria today likely has the largest number of Westerners in any jihadist battlefield in the modern era, with greater numbers of Western participants than in past battlefields in Afghanistan (including during the 1980s anti-Soviet

---

[1] The opinions and conclusions expressed in this testimony are the author's alone and should not be interpreted as representing those of RAND or any of the sponsors of its research. This product is part of the RAND Corporation testimony series. RAND testimonies record testimony presented by RAND associates to Federal, State, or local legislative committees; Government-appointed commissions and panels; and private review and oversight bodies. The RAND Corporation is a non-profit research organization providing objective analysis and effective solutions that address the challenges facing the public and private sectors around the world. RAND's publications do not necessarily reflect the opinions of its research clients and sponsors.

[2] This testimony is available for free download at *http://www.rand.org/pubs/testimonies/CT414.html*.

war), Pakistan, Iraq (including after the 2003 U.S. invasion), Somalia, Yemen, and Libya.[3] But it is important not to exaggerate the threat. Westerners appear to be involved in a range of activities, from providing humanitarian aid to fighting with al-Qaeda-affiliated groups like Jabhat al-Nusrah. It is unclear how many of these individuals will attempt to return to the United States and become involved in terrorist activity. Some may die in Syria, some may move to other countries (including other jihadist battlefields), some may focus on humanitarian activity, and still others may become disillusioned with extremist activities. In addition, other groups, such as al-Qaeda in the Arabian Peninsula and core al-Qaeda, likely present a more immediate threat to the U.S. homeland—at least today. Still, the large number of Western violent extremists in sanctuaries like Syria makes it particularly important to adopt policies and practices in the U.S. homeland and overseas to ensure that violent extremists are detected if they return to the West and, more broadly, to reduce the flow of foreign fighters from the West.

I have divided my comments into four sections. The first provides an overview of the threat from sanctuaries in Syria and potentially Iraq. The second section provides broader context and analyzes trends in the number of Salafi-jihadist groups, fighters, and attacks. The third examines the impact of this threat on the U.S. homeland. And the fourth section explores measures to detect and interdict the movement of Western violent extremists—including Americans—and prevent them from conducting attacks in the West.

THE THREAT FROM SANCTUARIES IN SYRIA AND IRAQ

The United States faces a threat from violent extremists traveling to—and returning from—Syria and other locations. Since 2011, between 100 and 200 Americans have traveled—or attempted to travel—to Syria to assist rebel organizations. There appear to be a wide range of motivations, such as conducting violent jihad, fighting Shi'a, supporting Syrian nationalist groups against the Assad regime, and providing humanitarian assistance. However, the problem is broader than just Americans. Between 1,500 and 2,500 Sunni extremists from Europe arrived in Syria between January 2012 and July 2014. Many have joined jihadist groups such as Jabhat al-Nusrah and the Islamic State of Iraq and al-Sham (ISIS). In turn, between 300 and 400 extremists appear to have left Syria for countries in Europe.[4] There are also a growing number of other Westerners, including Australians, participating in such jihadist battlefields as Syria. With the increase in ISIS control of territory in Iraq, there may be a growing number of Western violent extremists in Iraq as well.

These developments should cause concern in the United States. European travelers do not need a visa to enter the United States. This is generally not a problem for known violent extremists that make it onto European—and then American—terrorism watch lists. But it is a problem if terrorist fighters and supporters train in Syria without being detected and, consequently, without making it onto any watch list. U.S. and European intelligence collection capabilities are not as robust in Syria today as they were in Iraq and Afghanistan, but the number of Western violent extremists appears to be significantly greater.

BROADER TRENDS

The problem of violent extremism is broader than just Syria and Iraq. Current trends suggest that terrorist groups are metastasizing, particularly in North Africa and the Middle East. As noted in the next section, however, many of these groups are not a high threat to the United States today and are focused on local enemies.

Figure 1 shows the number of active Salafi-jihadist groups, including al-Qaeda, by year since 1988. Salafi-jihadist groups can be distinguished by at least two main characteristics. First, these groups emphasize the importance of returning to a "pure" Islam, that of the Salaf, the pious ancestors. Second, Salafi-jihadist groups believe that violent jihad is fard 'ayn (a personal religious duty). Al-Qaeda leader Ayman al-Zawahiri, among others, encourages both Salafism and armed jihad.[5] Each data point on the y-axis in Figure 1 represents the number of active Salafi-jihadist groups that year. As highlighted in the figure, there was a steady increase

---

[3] Author estimates based on an overview of Salafi-jihadist groups and fighters since 1988. See, for example, Seth G. Jones, *A Persistent Threat: The Evolution of al-Qaeda and Other Salafi Jihadists* (Santa Monica, CA: RAND, 2014).

[4] Author interviews with senior counterterrorism and diplomatic officials from a dozen European countries, July 2014.

[5] On the term Salafi-jihadists see, for example, Assaf Moghadam, "Motives for Martyrdom: Al-Qaida, Salafi Jihad, and the Spread of Suicide Attacks," *International Security*, Vol. 33, No. 3, Winter 2008/09, pp. 46–78; Moghadam, "The Salafi-Jihad as a Religious Ideology," *CTC Sentinel*, Vol. 1, No. 3, February 2008, pp. 14–16.

in the number of groups during the 1990s and 2000s, but a notable jump in the slope of the line after 2010. Most of these new groups were in North Africa and the Levant.[6]

FIGURE 1: NUMBER OF SALAFI-JIHADIST GROUPS BY YEAR, 1988–2013 [7]

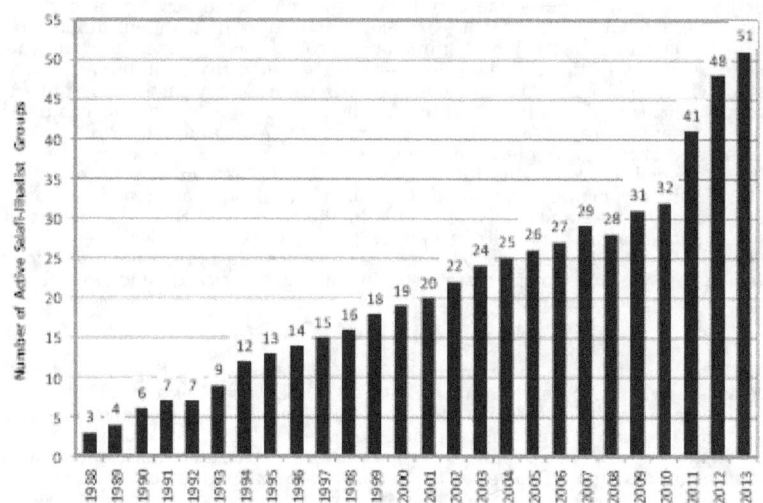

Figure 2 provides a rough estimate of the number of Salafi-jihadist fighters between 1988 and 2013. Calculating the number of Salafi-jihadists is difficult, in part since groups do not provide public estimates of their numbers and they can vary considerably over the course of a group's life. Consequently, Figure 2 includes high and low estimates for the number of Salafi-jihadists by year. The trend is similar to Figure 1. There was a notable increase in the number of fighters after 2010. The biggest jump was in Syria, which witnessed a dramatic rise in the number of fighters.

---

[6] As used here, Levant refers to the area that includes Syria, Jordan, Lebanon, Israel, Palestine, and southern Turkey.

[7] Jones, *A Persistent Threat*, p. 27.

FIGURE 2: NUMBER OF SALAFI-JIHADISTS BY YEAR, 1988–2013 [8]

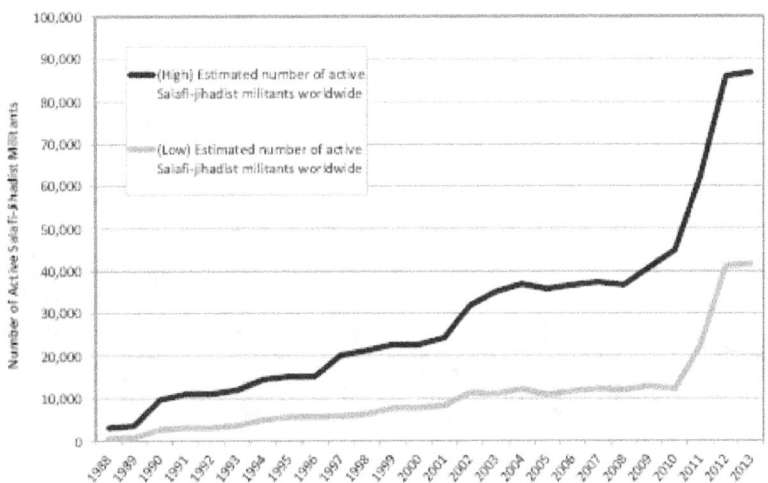

Figure 3 highlights the number of attacks by core al-Qaeda and affiliates since 2009.[9] The data indicate a substantial rise in the number of attacks over time. Trends for casualties and fatalities were similar. There was a 167 percent increase in attacks by al-Qaeda-affiliated groups between 2010 and 2013, with most of the violence in 2013 perpetrated by ISIS (44 percent), Jabhat al-Nusrah (24 percent), al-Shabaab (22 percent), and al-Qaeda in the Arabian Peninsula (9 percent). This marked a change from 2012, when al-Shabaab conducted the most attacks (46 percent).

---

[8] Jones, *A Persistent Threat*, p. 27.

[9] The data on attacks by other Salafi-jihadist groups were much less reliable, so I have not included the number of attacks by Salafi-jihadists outside of al-Qaeda.

FIGURE 3: NUMBER OF ATTACKS BY AL-QAEDA AND AFFILIATES, 2009–2013 [10]

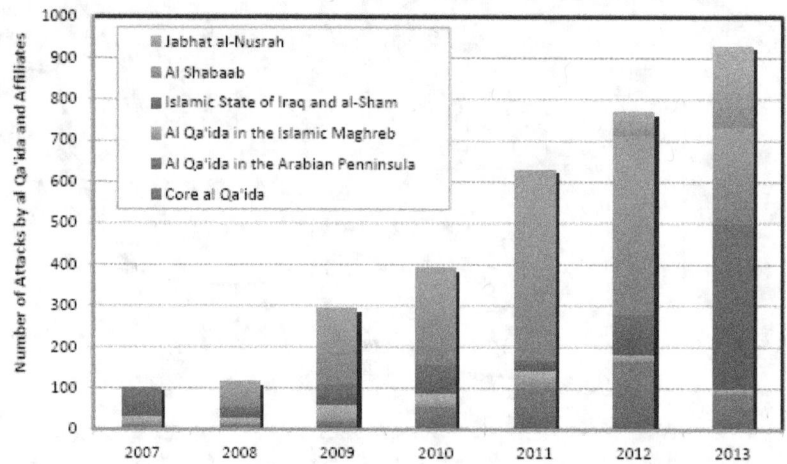

To summarize the data, there was a 55 percent increase in the number of Salafi-jihadist groups from 2010 to 2013, primarily in North Africa and the Levant. Libya represents the most active sanctuary for Salafi-jihadist groups in North Africa, and Syria the most significant safe haven for groups in the Levant. In addition, the number of Salafi-jihadists roughly doubled from 2010 to 2013, according to both low and high estimates. The war in Syria was the single most important attraction for Salafi-jihadist fighters.

These trends suggest that the United States needs to remain focused on countering the proliferation of violent extremist groups, including Salafi-jihadists, despite the temptation to shift attention and resources to other regions and to significantly decrease counterterrorism budgets in an era of fiscal constraint.

IMPACT ON THE U.S. HOMELAND

Not all terrorist groups overseas present a direct threat to the U.S. homeland. As Table 1 highlights, terrorist groups can be divided into three categories: Those that pose a high threat because they are involved in active plotting against the U.S. homeland; groups that pose a medium threat because they are involved in plotting attacks against U.S. structures like embassies and U.S. citizens overseas (though not against the U.S. homeland); and those that pose a low threat because they are focused on targeting local regimes or other countries.

---

[10] Data are based on author estimates and the Jane's Terrorism and Insurgency Intelligence Centre Events Database.

TABLE 1.—EXAMPLE OF TERRORISTS THAT THREATEN THE UNITED STATES

	High Threat	Medium Threat	Low Threat
Characteristics ...	Active plotting against the U.S. homeland and U.S. targets overseas (e.g. U.S. embassies and citizens).	Active plotting against U.S. targets overseas (e.g. U.S. embassies and citizens).	Limited or no active plotting against U.S. targets overseas.
Examples	• al-Qaeda in the Arabian Peninsula. • Core al-Qaeda ..... • Some inspired individuals and networks.	• Al Shabaab .... • Jabhat al-Nusrah • ISIS .... • Ansar al-Sharia Libya. • Hezbollah	• East Turkestan Islamic Movement. • Suqor al-Sham.

First, some groups pose a high threat. Al-Qaeda in the Arabian Peninsula and possibly core al-Qaeda likely present the most immediate threat, along with inspired networks and individuals. The growth in social media and the terrorist use of chat rooms, Facebook, Twitter, YouTube, and other sites has facilitated radicalization inside the United States.

Second, there are a number of groups that pose a medium threat. Al-Shabaab's objectives are largely parochial, and it has conducted attacks in Somalia and the region. But al-Shabaab possesses a competent external operations capability to strike targets outside of Somalia. The Westgate Mall attack in Nairobi, Kenya was well-planned and well-executed, and involved sophisticated intelligence collection, surveillance, and reconnaissance of the target.[11]

ISIS and Jabhat al-Nusrah are primarily interested in establishing Islamic emirates in Iraq, Syria, and the broader region, though their growing networks in Europe and the United States are concerning. Their access to foreign fighters, external network in Europe, and bomb-making expertise suggest that they may already have the capability to plan and support attacks against the West. It is currently unclear whether most of these individuals will remain in Syria or Iraq over the long run, move to other war zones, or return to the West. And even if some return, it is uncertain whether they will become involved in terrorist plots, focus on recruiting and fundraising, or become disillusioned with terrorism. Still, foreign fighters have historically been agents of instability. They can affect the conflicts they join, as they did in post-2003 Iraq by promoting sectarian violence and indiscriminate tactics. Perhaps more important, foreign fighter mobilizations empower transnational terrorist groups such as al-Qaeda, because volunteering for war is the principal stepping-stone for individual involvement in more extreme forms of militancy. When Muslims in the West radicalize, they usually do not plot attacks in their home country right away, but travel to a war zone first. A majority of al-Qaeda operatives began their militant careers as war volunteers, and most transnational jihadi groups today are by-products of foreign fighter mobilizations.[12]

Third, some groups present a low-level threat to the United States. They do not possess the capability or intent to target the United States at home or overseas. They include such groups as the East Turkestan Islamic Movement, which has a support base among China's Uighur community and is primarily interested in Chinese targets. Despite this categorization, there is some fluidity between levels because the capabilities and intentions of groups—and their leadership—evolve over time.

DETECTING AND DETERRING TRAVELERS

U.S. intelligence, law enforcement, military, and diplomatic officials have spent considerable time and resources on understanding the threat and developing measures to counter the spread of violent extremists from sanctuaries like Syria. But the

---

[11] Committee on Homeland Security, *Al-Shabaab: Recruitment and Radicalization Within the Muslim American Community and the Threat to the Homeland, Majority Investigative Report* (Washington, DC: U.S. House of Representatives, July 27, 2011), p. 2.

[12] Thomas Hegghammer, "The Rise of Muslim Foreign Fighters: Islam and the Globalization of Jihad," *International Security*, Vol. 35, No. 3, Winter 2010/11, pp. 53–94.

situation is complex. Violent extremists usually don't advertise that they plan to fight in battlefields like Syria, and many attempt to take circuitous routes to Syria rather flying directly from the United States to neighboring countries like Turkey. Moving forward, the United States should consider several additional measures to detect and deter violent extremists from coming to—or departing from—the United States.

Working with Europe.—The first is to continue assisting European allies, including Turkey, in efforts to identify violent extremists traveling to—and from—jihadist battlefields like Syria. U.S. and European intelligence collection capabilities are not as robust in Syria today as they were in Iraq and Afghanistan, but the number of Western violent extremists is greater.

European states have taken some steps against jihadists traveling to—and from—Syria and Iraq. The United Kingdom, Germany, Belgium, France, the Netherlands, Spain, Norway, and several other countries have arrested some outgoing and returning fighters, facilitators, and recruiters. In addition, several European countries have stripped their welfare benefits, frozen their financial assets, and seized their passports to prevent further travel. The United Kingdom, in particular, has established robust measures. In June 2014, the United Kingdom passed legislation banning ISIS and four other Syria-linked extremist groups, giving it the ability to prosecute individuals associated with or supporting these groups. The United Kingdom is one of only seven European countries that can seize passports of Syria-bound travelers not charged with a separate offense.

The United States should continue working with its allies to improve European counterterrorism and counter-radicalization measures in several areas:

- *Regional intelligence-sharing.*—Increased counterterrorism intelligence sharing across Europe would strengthen regional awareness of returnees and Syria-based plotters. But some European states appear to be reluctant to implement comprehensive intelligence-sharing mechanisms across Europe because of data privacy, data protection, and other concerns. Improved European Union approaches to the foreign fighter problem, including strengthening Schengen area border security and expanding the use of the EUROPOL and INTERPOL notice system, would enhance European states' ability to mitigate the threat.[13]
- *Attendance at terrorist camps.*—Criminalizing attendance (not just training) at terrorist camps overseas would likely deter some terrorists from traveling to Syria and Iraq, as well as allow states to prosecute more returnees. It is likely an easier charge to prove than receiving terrorist training. The United Kingdom is the only European Union country with such a law. The United States prohibits attendance at terrorist camps overseas.
- *Pre-emptive action.*—Once individuals arrive in Syria and Iraq, it is already late in the radicalization process for those committed to violent extremism. If there are adequate legal grounds to arrest individuals before they travel to Syria or Iraq, however, it would be helpful. Norway, Netherlands, and France are among the few European countries that have preemptively arrested extremists preparing to travel to Syria.

Counterterrorism at Home.—The FBI, Department of Homeland Security, and State and local agencies have already increased efforts to counter the flow of violent extremists into—and out of—the United States. But the United States should consider a few additional counterterrorism steps. Following are two examples.

The first is to increase intelligence collection on potential American violent extremists traveling to—and from—Syria and to ensure that U.S. agencies (such as CIA, NSA, FBI, and DHS) are adequately resourced by Congress to collect, analyze, and process signals and human intelligence on such travel. Extremists from the United States or other countries with visa waiver access need to be placed on proper watch lists in the United States, Europe, and other countries. It is troubling, however, that U.S. citizen Moner Mohammad Abu-Salha traveled to Syria to fight with al-Qaeda-affiliated rebels, returned to the United States around May 2013 without U.S. officials realizing that he had trained with an al-Qaeda-linked group, and traveled back to Syria in November 2013 before blowing himself up in a suicide attack in May 2014. In short, U.S. officials apparently did not realize that a U.S. citizen who had received terrorist training in Syria was on American soil for approximately 6 months before returning to Syria to perpetrate a terrorist attack overseas. Was this a problem in U.S. intelligence collection or analysis overseas, information sharing with allies, customs and border protection inside the United States, law enforce-

---

[13] The Schengen area includes 26 European countries that have abolished passport and any other types of border control at their internal borders, permitting the free movement of individuals.

ment gaps inside the United States (including with violent extremists on the internet and social media), or something else?

Second, the United States should consider adopting—and Congress should consider studying and potentially funding—a modified version of the United Kingdom's bottom-up law enforcement approach to counterterrorism. In the United Kingdom, there is a counterterrorism coordinating officer in each local police force, ranging in size from one officer to several hundred in the Metropolitan Police Special Branch. This is the point of contact for counterterrorism in local communities.

The FBI and large U.S. police departments—such as Washington, New York, and Los Angeles—are better prepared for counterterrorism than most other departments. But terrorist plots are often hatched outside of these urban centers, and many of the Americans traveling to battlefields like Syria are apparently from rural or suburban areas. Moner Mohammad Abu-Salha lived for a time with his brother in Fort Pierce, Florida, 130 miles north of Miami. Najibullah Zazi constructed his bombs to attack the New York City subway in Aurora, Colorado. Faisal Shahzad rigged his dark blue Nissan Pathfinder with explosives in Connecticut, and then drove it to Times Square in New York City. Many smaller police forces are not involved in counterterrorism, understandably focusing on criminal activity and other local challenges. Their departments often aren't resourced, trained, or prepared to deal with violent extremists in their communities. Yet local law enforcement agencies have a permanent presence in cities and towns, and frequently a better understanding of local communities. As Bruce Hoffman argued in his book *Inside Terrorism*, a critical step in countering terrorist groups is for law enforcement officials to "develop strong confidence-building ties with the communities from which terrorists are most likely to come or hide in . . . The most effective and useful intelligence comes from places where terrorists conceal themselves and seek to establish and hide their infrastructure."[14]

One variant of the U.K. approach in the United States might be to consider appointing a counterterrorism representative in most police departments to act as the intelligence point of contact across the department for counterterrorism. Counterterrorism would not necessarily be the full-time responsibility of this individual or group, who might be more focused on dealing with drugs, homicides, or other local challenges. But this individual would be responsible for coordinating concerns about violent extremists in their community and improving outreach programs to businesses, ethnic communities, schools, and other locations. In addition to serving as the subject-matter expert on counterterrorism (including training and contingency planning), this individual would closely cooperate with local Joint Terrorism Task Forces and Fusion Centers. Many police agencies do not have a single point of contact for counterterrorism.

It is important to take proactive steps now to deal with the problem of terrorist sanctuaries. After all, the threat from violent extremists will persist. As a poem entitled "Mujahid's Wish" in the Spring 2013 issue of al-Qaeda's *Inspire* magazine highlighted, the United States remains a bitter enemy:

"I wish I am in America. It seems odd, right?
Hijra is not the end of a mujahid's ambition.
Walking with an AK is not the end of the road. I used
To think the same as you, until I met brothers in the
Training camps, brothers who look into the enemies'
Barrels and see Jannah. Surprisingly, many of them
Wish to live in America. They have one gentle project
To carry out; detonating even one bomb in any crowded
area. They wish to be lone mujahideen like Tamerlan.
Many of the brothers who made Hijrah from the West
Wish they have a return ticket, returning home
Heading for mom's kitchen. Not to serve the kuffar
With delicious and exotic meals, but to terrorize the
American society until they case to fight and assault Muslims.
Brother residing in the West, grab your chance and
Walk steadfastly towards your goal.
As for me here in Yemen, whenever I move around with
Explosives around my waist, I wish I am in America."[15]

---

[14] Bruce Hoffman, *Inside Terrorism*, Second Edition (New York: Columbia University Press, 2006), p. 169.

[15] Sheikh Ibrahim Ar-Rubaysh, "Allah Will Restrain the Evil Might of Those Who Disbelieve," *Inspire*, Spring 1434, 2013, No. 11, pp. 36–37.

Mr. KING. Let me thank all of the witnesses for their testimony. I am going to have two questions. I will ask them both and then just ask if each of the four panelists could give their thoughts on them.

One is, we talk about ISIS and we talk about AQAP, et cetera, the various groups. If you could give evidence or testimony on how much cross-pollination there is, like how strictly are these lines of demarcation enforced? Or would you find an AQAP bomb-maker, for instance, lending his services to ISIS? Again, since the command structure of al-Qaeda seems to have broken down, how strictly is the demarcation enforced among the other groups? That would be the first question.

Then, second, Dr. Jones mentioned the—how this appears to be—not appears—it would seem to be just by number-wise much more of a threat to Europe than it is to the United States. Now, we are probably the ultimate target, but as far as numbers, there are thousands and thousands of Europeans. If you could address the question of not just what laws have been passed, but how seriously, other than the Brits, are European governments and nations facing this issue of the returning foreign fighters? So we will start with Dr. Kagan and just work our way across. Thank you.

Mr. KAGAN. Thank you, Mr. Chairman.

There is a tremendous amount of cross-pollination among the groups. I am not persuaded that the command of al-Qaeda has broken down. It depends on what you thought the command of al-Qaeda was to begin with. It has always been a rather loosely-affiliated organization.

What we have seen is Zawahiri actually effecting more command and control publicly of it, especially with the mediation between ISIS and JN, than we usually had seen. But what is important to understand is that the leaders of these groups represent a human network that has—that for the most part goes back decades. A lot of these guys fought together against the Soviets. They have been fighting together against us for the 1990s. They know each other.

We should remember that Naser al-Wuhayshi, the head of al-Qaeda in the Arabian Peninsula, is also the operational commander for Zawahiri at this point. We have seen cooperation between Shabaab and AQAP. We have these very credible reports of cooperation between AQAP and Jabhat Nusra. We have reports of cooperation between AQIM and Boko Haram.

This is a movement. It is a global movement. Its organizations are complex, but we should not imagine that these organizations are in any way stovepiped from each other.

Mr. KING [continuing]. European government concern and action?

Mr. KAGAN. It is beyond my area of expertise to talk much about that, except to say that the European focus on privacy, to the exclusion of all other considerations, is making Europe a very effective cyber safe haven, among other things, for malign actors of all varieties, and we are seeing an increase of migration of malign cyber activity to European servers because they cannot by law inspect any of the packets or things that go in and out of those servers.

Mr. KING. With that comment regarding Europe, we will go to Mr. Simcox from Europe.

Mr. SIMCOX. I will start with Europe. I think that there is certainly a recognition that it is a very, very dangerous situation, and the foreign fighters returning to Europe are going to pose a great problem. The shootings in the Jewish Museum in Brussels, we have already displayed that that is very clearly the case.

Where the European countries are very much lacking, I think, is two aspects; one, the legislation. Dr. Jones referred to this already, and it is a problem in terms of preparatory offenses, that—it is easy to obviously take action after a terrorist attack has taken place, but some of these preparatory ones, European governments aren't well-fitted-out legislatively to deal with them.

In the United Kingdom, we had to pass a lot of laws to begin to effectively counter this. We still haven't really got it exactly right, but we have been more serious than others on taking very stringent actions against those who are preparing for terrorist attacks, not just in the United Kingdom, but increasingly abroad.

But I do think they have a problem with political will, as well, because, look, a lot of these countries, they hear about the problem more than they see it, in terms of it has only been the United Kingdom and Spain that have really suffered extremely badly in terms of loss of life in Europe from terrorist groups.

There have been other small incidents in France and Belgium, but in terms of mass casualties, it is only the United Kingdom and Spain that have really suffered. I think that part of it is the very nature of the fact that there hasn't been the huge loss of life as there has in the United States and the United Kingdom to this kind of terrorism.

In terms of the cross-pollination, it certainly—it certainly happens, I would back up all Dr. Kagan said. The one thing maybe I would add to that is that one of the good things about the intensity of the U.S. drone campaign has been that perhaps some of these— let's say somebody like Ibrahim al-Asiri, the AQAP bomb-maker, it is very hazardous for him to try and put his head above the parapet and work too closely with groups outside of Yemen and those he trusts very closely in Yemen, because the huge amounts of attention that are based on people like that, because of U.S. drones and military operations is very high, which is why I think we need to keep the pressure on in situations like that so that even greater interaction between the groups doesn't take place.

Mr. KING. Dr. Brookes.

Mr. BROOKES. Yes, I think that Dr. Kagan has covered it quite well. I mean, we should be definitely concerned, this most recent plot regarding cell phones and electronic devices shows you the force multiplier effect that can take place. If you have a very skilled, innovative bomb-maker who might be working with willing travelers or willing terrorist operatives in al-Qaeda or Syria, I mean, this is very problematic to me.

We have seen the cross-pollination between AQIM and Boko Haram and al-Shabaab and AQAP, and now we are seeing it between AQAP and the Syria-Iraq theater of operation. I think this was a real wake-up call to us, and I think it may be the most imminent threat that we face today. It is going to be a very difficult summer.

My concern about Europe is that—and I mentioned a little bit in my testimony is that publicly, are we taking this threat seriously? Some of the rhetoric that has come out of the administration to me has been troubling and may be breeding a sense of complacency.

I think we are in a very much in a very difficult and dire situation here regarding this threat. I think that Europe and other parts or places around the world are watching the United States and looking for leadership on this issue. I think it is critically important that we have some sort of harmonization. International cooperation is critically important to fighting terrorism, whether you are talking about intelligence, legal, funding. I mean, terrorists still need funding to undertake operations and travel, so it is critically important.

I think despite the challenges we are facing with Europe right now with Russia, the Ukraine, and things along that line, that terrorism has to be a top priority for senior leadership in the United States to make the—to increase our security here and to our interests overseas.

Mr. KING. Thank you, Dr. Brookes.

Dr. Jones.

Mr. JONES. Sure, I will be brief. I realize I am in the red now. First, on the cross-pollination——

Mr. KING. Don't worry about that. Just go ahead.

Mr. JONES. Okay. In terms of al-Qaeda in the Arabian Peninsula and its role in the Syria-Iraq context, my own view is that its relationship is closest with Nusra, because Nusra is an al-Qaeda affiliate, along with AQAP, and the relationship between Naser al-Wuhayshi, the emir in Yemen, and the Jalani in Syria is the closest.

But I think what everybody said is right. The challenge here is that when you have so many foreign fighters coming from Europe, some in the United States, North Africa, Australia, they move between groups. So there are formal group members, but there is a lot of movement of individuals who aren't formally affiliated. So in that sense, this makes this more challenging than I think we have seen in some other battlefields.

On the European issue, I would just point to one challenge on the European context is that the Schengen agreement allows for the free movement of people within European Schengen countries. The fact that we have different laws, then, among these countries means that we have free movement, but we have different laws when people return or before they leave, so the challenge for us then is we don't have agreement across European countries, but we do have the free movement of people.

So I would say the United Kingdom has been and continues to be very concerned and has taken action and considers the threat seriously. The French and Spanish, in my view, have been very concerned, have conducted operations against Syrians and Spanish citizens in North Africa and Syria that they consider a threat, and there are several other countries, including the Norwegians now, have put laws in place that make it more difficult for people to travel to or to rest once they come back.

But I think outside of that, what we are seeing is huge variations. With visa waiver access into the United States, that should cause some concern here.

Mr. KING. Thank you. Ranking Member, Mr. Higgins.

Mr. HIGGINS. Thank you, Mr. Chairman.

Dr. Brookes, I just wanted to pick up on something that you had said relative to statements coming out of the White House and American policy in that part of the world. You know, the more you learn about that part of the world, the more you conclude that it is an absolute mess and that there are no good options for the United States.

I take you back to September, when the administration was looking for Congress to authorize some kind of unspecified military action in Syria, which I opposed, primarily because at that point it seemed as though, you know, the administration was using the justification that 100,000 people had been killed because of the use of chemical weapons in Syria.

Well, the most effective fighters on the other side were al-Qaeda affiliates and Islamic extremists who were beheading people that were supporting the government. When we looked to the rest of the world for support, including the 22-nation Arab League, they basically said, yeah, we will support the United States as long as we don't have to do anything. Out of 194 countries, we had explicit support from Turkey and France. That was basically it.

So my concern was—and I am very respectful of your position—I don't mean this to be antagonistic at all, I just—I want to probe it, to be truthful. You know, the United States would have essentially went in to litigate a civil war in that part of the world for the third time, essentially alone again. That to me is very troubling.

The United States gets played in that part of the world, whether it is the corrupt government in Afghanistan and its successor corrupt governments or whether it is the situation in Iraq. You know, someone had mentioned Qasem Soleimani, who is head of the Quds Forces, which as I understand it is essentially a cross between special forces and the CIA. You know, he cut the deal in Iran to give Nouri al-Maliki another term in office. So where do his loyalties lie?

You know, at some point, at some point, these countries have to take responsibility for their own future. The United States has a limited role here. You know, General Jack Keane and Dr. Kagan and so many others, you know, the surge in Iraq was intended to do one thing, really—tamp down violence to allow a breathing space within which the warring factions could reach political reconciliation, including the sharing of oil revenues, to peacefully coexist in that country toward the goal of forging some kind of semblance of democracy.

That has been an abject failure. Nouri al-Maliki was told at that time that unless and until he could reach into the Sunni community, the Kurd community, and instill a sense of confidence that he had the leadership ability to forge something better, we would end up with what we have. What we have is not our fault. The American military did everything possible and continues to in an advisory role to give them the opportunity to forge a better future.

But unless and until these two warring factions realize that, you know, the future is more important than these past grievances. So I went on a little bit, but, Dr. Brookes, go ahead.

Mr. BROOKES. I am not sure where to start with that, but thank you very much for sharing your thoughts. I mean, there are a lot of opportunities to go back and talk about hypothetical counterfactuals, if we had done something different, but we are where we are today. I think that is the critical point here, is that I assume that the panelists would agree with me—and I will let them speak for themselves—is that we are facing a dire threat in that part of the world that not only is a threat to U.S. interests— in a difficult part of the world—to U.S. interests, but also, I think, increasingly to the homeland and what do we do about that? I mean, I did talk about some things. Like I said, I wish we had done some things differently, but we can't go back and change that.

So we are really saying, how do we go forward here? I think that is the purpose of the panel here, and I think there have been some good ideas put out by my colleagues here about what we need to do, working with international partners to try to deal with us. I hope we can all agree that we have a significant problem and that it needs to be publicized. I think it needs to be—we need to look at international cooperation for help with it. Like I said, going back now, I am not saying it is not important, but it is—I think we have to see where we go forward now at this point to deal with the challenges that we are facing.

Mr. HIGGINS. Yield back.

Mr. KING. Gentleman yields back.

Dr. Broun, from Georgia.

Mr. BROUN. Thank you, Mr. Chairman.

When I was in the United States Marine Corps, I was taught to know your enemy. The President, as you know, of the United States has made statements that Dr. Brookes referred to. Osama is dead. Al-Qaeda is on the run. Just yesterday, the full committee had a follow up on the 9/11 Commission's recommendations. Some statements were made by my Democrat colleagues that basically supported this type of philosophy.

Dr. Brookes was talking during his testimony that referred to this poor concept, in my opinion, by this administration of what we are facing, and I think there are Members of Congress that also have this poor concept of what we need to be doing to deal with this asymmetrical threat.

Dr. Kagan in his testimony talked about that our intel community, as well as our military, is being decimated. Frankly, Dr. Kagan, I think we have had four administrations—two Republican and two Democrats—that have steadily degraded our defense capability. I find that reprehensible. I think all four have just steadily degraded our intel communities, as well.

It is boots on the ground that is going to be absolutely critical, particularly in these safe havens, for us to know what kind of threats that we are actually facing. So I applaud your testimony, Dr. Kagan, about that, and I hope the administration is listening to you guys, all four of you, because I think it is absolutely critical, because we are not facing as a Nation the threat that we face, this asymmetric threat.

Now, as a person who believes in the Constitution that our founding fathers meant for it to be, the major function of the Federal Government should be National defense and National security. We don't have enough ships in the Navy, we don't have enough wings in the Air Force, we don't have enough brigades in the Army, and I can tell you, as a U.S. Marine, God knows we don't have enough Marines.

We are paring the defense capability down, but beyond that, we have got a lot of state threats around the world, and we have all these asymmetric threats with these safe havens. What I would like for you all to do—and my question to you is, what would you tell the administration, what can we do?

The other follow-up question for all four of you is this. When you have a snake, the way to kill the snake is cut off his head. The greatest amount of financing—I believe is coming from Iran. What would you do to help—each one of you—to help cut off the head of the supply chain, not only from Iran, but I know that from our committee work here that there is financing coming from the United States actually to help all these al-Qaeda-like organizations around the world.

We have got a tremendous problem. We have got to stop worrying about containment, in my opinion, and start cutting off the head of the snake and end this once and for all, because we are going to be here spending trillions of dollars over the next decades, maybe century, if we don't do something about it.

So what is your solution? We will start with Dr. Kagan.

Mr. KAGAN. I can't give you a solution in a minute-and-a-half or even in quite a few minutes.

Mr. BROUN. Well, you can answer about——

Mr. KAGAN. I will answer your question.

Mr. BROUN. No, I am talking about written answers. I would appreciate all of you all——

Mr. KAGAN. I am going to have to ask for quite a bit of time on that.

Mr. BROUN. Okay, please do.

Mr. KAGAN. This is a very complicated problem, and there are no easy solutions. I think that the Ranking Member very articulately put the problem, but I think—and it is something that is paralyzing to a lot of people as they think about it. This is an insanely complicated problem; it really is. We don't have good options. Almost all of the options that we are looking at are various degrees of bad or worse.

But if it were the case that these problems were confined to the region, we might be able to say that, you know, this is too hard, this is too complicated, we don't have support, they need to stand up. The problem is that the threats are to us. We must act against them, lest they act against us.

So we have to address the complexity of this. It is out of respect for that complexity that I am not going to answer directly what a strategy would be—we are working on this. Everyone here at the table is working on it. We are working on it at AEI. We are trying to come up with something.

But, frankly, there is not a lot of appetite in this administration for strategy, because we are still having arguments about whether

38

or not there is a problem. So the first thing that we need to do is what this committee is already doing, which is to recognize and publicize the extent of the threat and the extent of the problem and say we need to deal with it.

What I will tell you is, we should immediately reverse the defense cuts. I agree with you that this has been a bipartisan attack on defense going back to the first Bush administration. We need to stop the runaway train toward curtailing our intelligence activities and impose appropriate oversight and appropriate controls to prevent abuses, while simultaneously enhancing our intelligence capabilities to understand this threat and help us develop strategies for it.

These are two things that I think Congress can really take the lead on that would be extremely important and that will set the stage and create conditions that will make it possible to execute a coherent strategy as we can try to develop one and hopefully ultimately get an administration that would be willing to do so.

Mr. BROOKES. Could I add to that? I mean, I agree with that. The other thing I would say is—and this may not surprise anybody based on my pedigree, but I am continually or increasingly concerned that we are unwilling to use military direct action in support of U.S. National interests.

I am not saying there is a military solution to this. I believe in using all of the instruments of National policy to solve problems, but I sense that there is—everybody doesn't really want to say that we shouldn't—you know, the talk about using airpower in Iraq, for instance, for dealing with—as one of the ways or tools we can deal with this issue. I am concerned that people are becoming increasingly worried or unlikely to support the idea that we may need to use military operations to support our National security. I think that is something we have to throw back on the table, along with the other instruments of National policy, as an option when we feel we are facing an increasing threat.

Mr. BROUN. Dr. Brookes, could I follow up real quickly, if I may, Mr. Chairman? I believe very firmly that SF, special forces and special ops, are probably the best option to utilize, as well as civilian intelligence community—I see Dr. Jones shaking his head agreeing with me—and I believe very firmly that we need to be expanding, not only our total defense capabilities, but I think we need to be expanding our special operations community.

Pushing it down even further out of active forces down into the Reserves and even into the Guard units, because I believe that is going to be the ultimate solution for military action in these kind of things.

I believe very firmly, we should never go to war unless Congress declares war. Congress has not done its duty in—through the Authorization for Use of Military Force and the War Powers Act of controlling Presidents of either party.

But, Dr. Jones, you shook your head. Agree?

Mr. JONES. Yes, two follow-on points. No. 1 is, I think we have got to be very careful when we talk about this threat that we then don't take actions that undermine our seriousness. If we talk about this threat, if we talk—if our policymakers talk about the importance of counterterrorism missions, but then at the same time we are leaving Afghanistan and, by part of that, Pakistan, where we have core al-Qaeda that continues to operate, we have got a milieu of militant groups, I would just ask, how serious are we, then, if we are leaving one of the areas where we see the sort-of headquarters and—I don't want to overstate this—of the core, Ayman al-Zawahiri. So one thing I would say is, we cannot leave after 2016 unless these kinds of groups have been defeated or severely weakened.

The second issue that I would like to see more of, and I don't see it much right now, is a specific strategy to deal with the kinds of issues we are talking about today. What are the areas of the world that we see the most significant threats from, including this one we are talking about here today in the Syria-Iraq, and what resources are we going to put there?

Are we going to put in those areas then our sufficient signals intelligence collection capabilities, HUMINT, special operations forces, efforts to counter the ideology? What I don't—what I see missing right now—and I would say this with the last administration to some degree, as well—is a specific strategy with resources attached to it to deal with it.

I think until we see that, something we saw Reagan do effectively in 1981 and 1982 to deal with the Soviets, I don't think—I think we are going to continue to find problems as these jihadists groups pop up in a range of different places. So I would like to see a strategy, resources put against it, and see that communicated to the American public.

Mr. BROUN. Thank you, Mr. Chairman.

Mr. KING. The gentleman yields back. Now the newest Member of the committee and the newest Member of Congress, the gentleman from Florida, Mr. Clawson, is recognized.

Mr. CLAWSON. Everybody is going to be able to say that until November. Then I am going to have a little leg up.

I apologize for being late. I have found in this job that you become totally over-scheduled from your first day. So I am—in my world previous—was not accustomed to showing up late when people are going to speak. I hope you all don't take it the wrong way and just really appreciate you all being here. I have learned a lot. You know a lot. So I appreciate your service to the country.

I don't come at this in a partisan way. I will say that I believe that the Middle East is out of control. Whatever president or whatever is accosted, is of no service to me right now, because I think one of you said the cliche, "We are where we are." Correct, gentlemen?

I come at a little bit different. I believe that in this case, the supply chain is more important than the manufacturing site. The manufacturing site may well be Syria, Iraq, or Iran. But the supply chain for the next bomb into our country, I believe, runs through the heart of Europe, as you have spoken to.

I have lived in Spain and I have seen the immigrant population explode from northern Africa. I have seen the sealed garbage cans in the subways of Paris when I lived there. I have managed plants as far east as Turkey in the Islamic world.

These are troubled places. I also understand the point that you made earlier that these—although the European community is one entity in terms of borders, in terms of security, every country is so different from the other one. So I don't know how we manage that from afar, because it feels like if the wrong person gets on a plane to Barcelona, he can get to New York. He can get to New York.

So, therefore, my concern drilling down is: What do we do as a country? These are proud countries in Europe, and they are our partners. But what can we do to influence that situation so that they are more effective? Second, as a Member of this committee and a Member of the Foreign Relations Committee, what can Congress do and what can we do to help you so that we are more safe, relative to what goes on in Europe? Because I think another event could be just around the corner.

Gentlemen.

Mr. SIMCOX. Yes, if I could begin, and also I would just like to quickly comment on Congressman Broun's question, as well, if possible. I think the key thing—the United States has to take the lead in this. It really has to take the lead, and we—and a lot of Europe will take its direction from the United States.

On something like—Attorney General Holder talked about the—was in Norway recently talking about the need for European nations to toughen up certain parts of their legislation, which they currently aren't doing. The United States, you have this material support law which enables you to cover a huge variety of terrorism offenses that in Europe just doesn't exist.

So I think that there has to be a level of grave seriousness from the administration in terms of the way it talks about this threat. I think at the moment, still, the penny hasn't really dropped with the threat that Syria poses to the United States and Europe. There was a very unhelpful contribution from the former head of MI6 recently where he talked about how this could potentially be overblown. I think there is a danger we get complacent about the threat to the homeland, because there has not been a 9/11-style attack, obviously, on that scale since then.

Just to quickly go back to the defense question, I think this is another area where the United States has to take the lead, because other NATO countries are cutting defense spending even quicker than you are. There is this—this terrible notion of smart power that is upheld if everybody cut in different ways that we could somehow—the end result of that that we would all be safer is one that has taken root in Europe.

The United Kingdom does all it can. We have been of limited help in Iraq and Libya and Afghanistan, but where is the help from the rest of Europe in these kind of military interventions? It is few and far between, really.

So, again, I think if America starts cutting its military, that is a signal to Europe that it looks for excuses to do so, as well. So I really think strong American leadership is needed——

Mr. CLAWSON. Do we have unified conversations with European countries about the security risks so that there is a unified effort?

Mr. SIMCOX. Do those conversations take place? I believe they do from government to government, but I have not seen any—I would prefer to see some kind of collective announcement. It all seems very piecemeal at the moment, because European countries take the level of threat from the returnees from Syria very differently.

So at the moment, I don't think there is anything beyond just the cooperation that took place on counterterrorism efforts anyway, and Syria is a whole new load of casework.

Mr. CLAWSON. But then you would agree that the European security and, therefore, our security is dependent on the weakest link in the chain in the European community?

Mr. SIMCOX. Absolutely.

Mr. CLAWSON. If that doesn't create the biggest problem here that we have, I don't know what does.

Mr. SIMCOX. Certainly.

Mr. CLAWSON. Because we are not going to shut it down in Syria or Iran all of a sudden. So the pipeline to us is through the weakest link in Europe. To your words, there are some countries that are not taking it as seriously.

Mr. SIMCOX. I believe so.

Mr. CLAWSON. Well, anything we can do? If you would like to communicate with me privately, I am very interested in this. I am not interested in partisanship. I am interested in preventing this problem or anything I can do as a Member of Congress in preventing this problem. Hope you all don't——

Mr. JONES. Yes, I just wanted to add, just to make sure when we talk about Europe, that we are also adding probably the most vulnerable and potentially the weakest link, which is not an E.U. country, but is a NATO country, and that is Turkey. The concern I have with Turkey is the vast majority of foreign fighters that are going into and coming out of Syria, as well as Iraq, are coming through Turkey. They are getting there by land, by air, and by sea.

So what I would like to see a little bit more fidelity on is, how much information is being passed by the Turks to the Europeans and to us about names of individuals with American passports and European passports going into and out of Turkey for—or into Syria in particular? So I would just—this is—in my view, this is not just a Europe or at least an E.U. issue. Turkey remains a very—because of its location next to Syria, a very, very important and potentially weak link.

Mr. CLAWSON. Turkey's economic future depends on manufacturing exports to Europe and tourism in the GNC. We have—the Europeans have leverage on the Turks. In spite of the administration that is in Turkey right now, the country is cut in half, that leverage exists back to the point if there is a European unified effort to lock down the pipeline, I believe Turkey would come along. Their future depends on it. Would you agree with that?

Mr. JONES. Yes.

Mr. CLAWSON. So anything you all can pass on to me about how we can improve the effort among the European community to make the entrance of terrorists safer, I would appreciate it. I am sorry if I have taken so much time here.

Mr. KING. The gentleman yields back.

In view of what we have heard as far as the foreign fighters to Europe and, you know, the weak links, do any of you have any thoughts about rethinking visa waiver, modifying it, adjusting it to the current situation?

Mr. SIMCOX. I mean, I couldn't speak to it with any great level of gravitas. I think there is, obviously, a great concern about the amount of traffic that goes between the United States and Europe, and we are right to be concerned about the potential threat. I suppose that the one thing I would caution against is going over the top on it. In terms of the actual numbers, I mean, 2,000 is—which is a potential amount that have gone from Europe—is an awful lot, and it is a potential threat.

But in terms of the overall picture of the amount of travel between Europe and the United States that does take place, I wouldn't want to see a significant strain on relations because of an issue like that.

Mr. BROOKES. Mr. Chairman, the only thing I would add, I would suggest you may want to talk to some of the people at Heritage who deal with visa waiver issues more deeply than I do, have a great level of expertise, but my concern is, is that we should extend our defense perimeter as far away from the United States as possible and beyond Europe.

I think we—I am not convinced—and unfortunately, I didn't have an opportunity to see the House Foreign Affairs Committee yesterday hearing on Iraq, but I would want to know as a committee Member what the strategy is for dealing with, you know, the inside strategy, the Classified strategy for dealing with what is going on in Syria and Iraq and the rise of ISIS and other al-Qaeda-related groups.

I mean, I think we need—we would want to be dealing with it at that distance, not thinking about it at our shoreline or in Europe, as a portal. So—and I am—it is not clear to me—and, of course, I am outside the Government—that we have a comprehensive strategy for dealing with the rising threat that arises from groups like ISIS and al-Nusra and other militants in that part of that world. So I hope that the administration is speaking with you about those issues, but that is where I would want my first line of defense would be in theater, and I think that is where it needs to be, as opposed to in Europe, or at our shoreline.

Mr. KING. I guess the concern I would have is, how certain are we as to how certain the European nations are about who the Syrian foreign fighters are and to what level are they recording that and making that known to us and making it available to airline security?

Mr. KAGAN. Mr. Chairman, I think these are very good questions. I think I would go back to the issue of intelligence, because you are asking an intelligence question. The issue with visa is a visa—requiring someone to get a visa is only relevant if we have enough information to be able to say that we should or should not bring that person in. The more that we curtail our intelligence capabilities, the more it doesn't matter whether we have a Visa Waiver Program or not, because we won't have the intelligence that we need to put the pieces together to stop terrorists from getting our own visas.

This is a problem that we are having in Europe. I think one of the other problems that we are having is that the enormous damage that the traitor Snowden did to our National security includes driving a very powerful wedge between us and our European partners on the subject of intelligence sharing, working together, and that is something that needs to be taken on very directly and very energetically. It is not going to be taken on by apologizing to Angela Merkel about listening to her cell phone, which is not anyone's issue and also not a surprise to Angela Merkel, I suspect.

It is something that we need to take head-on. Again, it is why I say the specifics of what is being done to our intelligence capabilities are very important, but the overall messaging that is coming out of this country right now is that we are more interested in chasing after the possibility that a small number of people in the intelligence community might be doing things that they shouldn't be doing that are already illegal than we are about building up and supporting our capabilities to identify exactly the people that you worried about.

If that is our tone, we are going to have a very hard time getting the Europeans to take this intelligence problem very seriously. So my concern is less will they tell us, and more will they know? I think that is something that we really need to focus on.

Mr. SIMCOX. I would just add to that. We absolutely do not know. We don't know who all these—we don't know—I mean, the fact that we are estimating in the United Kingdom about the amount of people who have gone means we almost certainly don't know the amount of people who have come back. To give you an idea of the scale of this, I mean, in the United Kingdom, we have a relatively large intelligence budget, but nothing compared to the United States. There was a speech given a few years ago by the director general of MI5 who said that the United Kingdom monitors around 2,000 terrorist suspects. The threat has remained reasonably constant since then.

If you are talking about potentially 500 returnees from Syria—now, I know there won't be 500. Some will have died over there. Some may not come back. Some may not pose an absolute direct threat. But that is potentially about a quarter of MI5's case work just being added on in one conflict. There isn't the capacity in any way, shape, or form to begin to deal with that, even if we knew who all the people were, and we don't, which is why it is such a great problem for us.

Mr. KING. Okay. Dr. Jones.

Mr. JONES. I think the political and economic relationship—and even the military one with the Europeans is important and will continue to be important. I think rethinking visa waiver in general probably would not be helpful over the long run. I mean, there may be ways to work on trying to close gaps in laws that allow individuals from moving to or coming back from Syria, but I agree with what a number of people here have said. The issue is getting names on watch lists.

Look, our presence in Syria—even the U.S. presence is not like what it was in Afghanistan after the overthrow of the Taliban regime. It is not like what it was in Iraq. The jihadist problem is worse. We have much worse collection capabilities in these countries.

The issue I would also point out is, we have gotten it wrong, too. This is not just about the Europeans. We didn't get it right with the Tsarnaevs, the Boston bombers, who had traveled. We didn't get it right with Abu-Salah, who had gone to fight, come back, and then returned to blow himself up. We didn't catch Zazi going back and forth. We didn't catch Shizad going back and forth. So we continue to have similar issues with Americans going over and returning, as well.

So, you know, I think we also cannot forget that we have got issues with putting the right people on our watch lists, as well as pointing fingers at the Europeans.

Mr. BROOKES. I think, Mr. Chairman, we also—and I am sure this committee is obviously concerned about this and looking at it— is the lone wolf that is already here that may be inspired by what is going on there and never travels abroad. Obviously, that is always a concern to us, but this—what is going on, as I mentioned in my testimony, I think the establishment of this caliphate is going to be inspirational to many Islamists around the world on a number of different levels. I don't know what effect it will have, whether it brings in more foot soldiers or brings in more funding, brings in alliances. Of course, there probably will be some that will oppose it, as well, but that is another thing we have to worry about is the inspiration of Osama bin Laden's ideology and al-Qaeda's ideology for people wherever they are.

Mr. KING. All right, thank you.

The Ranking Member.

Mr. HIGGINS. Yes, just—you know, to what extent does the panel—I say this generally—believe that this is really a battle for control of that part of the world between Shia and Sunni that goes back to the 7th Century? Now, I was kind of intrigued, you know, the quick emergence of this Abu Bakr al-Baghdadi, you know, where would this guy come from? Why is he so extreme to even be essentially shunned in some reports by al-Qaeda, that—I don't think anybody accepts that that is a benign organization.

If you look at the origins, Abu Bakr was, you know, head of the first caliphate. He was the rightful successor as Sunnis believe to the Prophet Muhammad. His daughter was married to the Prophet Muhammad. He was a companion of him.

You know, you see how—what he says about Shias, that they are apostates, that they are not true Muslims. Vali Nasr, in his book "The Shia Revival," said that Sunnis in Lebanon believe that Shias have tails. I just think what you have got going on here is a battle for control of the 1.6 million Muslim world, the vast majority of whom are Sunni, but Shia obviously control, you know, Iran and now Iraq.

So, you know, what I am trying to figure out my own view of things is, can you allow that battle between these two groups to proceed and, at the same time, concurrently protect the homeland by use of military and intelligence? But I will leave it to the panel.

Mr. KAGAN. It is a great question, and it goes obviously to the heart of the complexity of the problem. There is now a sectarian war between Sunni and Shia that runs from the Persian Gulf to the Mediterranean and is expanding. I do not believe that that is a spontaneous development, and nor that it is a continuation of what—of—because, in fact, this is a worse and more widespread sectarian war than the Muslim world has seen for many, many centuries. This is an extreme aberration in that world. There have always been sectarian tensions, but organized sectarian warfare of this variety is extraordinarily rare in the Muslim community.

It is not accidental. It was caused in large part by the deliberate policies of Abu Bakr al-Baghdadi's predecessor, Abu Musab al-Zarqawi, who believed—apparently rightly—that it served his interests to stoke sectarian war in Iraq to try to get the Shia majority in Iraq to attack the Sunni minority in Iraq in order to drive recruitment for his cause, and that has been successful and it has spread and sectarian groups on both sides are leaning into this.

But the battle for the Muslim world that I am most concerned about is not the sectarian fight. It is the battle by al-Qaeda, which is an insurgent group fundamentally that does desire to gain control over the entire 1.6 million—or billion ummah to do so. I believe that its attempt will ultimately fail, because—and I am happy to have this conversation with you at greater length—this is part of the heresy that—what they espouse, in my view, part of a heresy that goes back to the very, very first days of Islam. It has emerged periodically. It is always rejected in the end by the Muslim community, and I believe that it will be rejected again here.

The question is: How long will it take? How much damage will be done in the mean time to the Muslims themselves and to us? But that is why I think that you can't separate the fight against al-Qaeda from the sectarian fight. We have to address both of those problems, and it is why we have to be careful—as one of my panelists said—not to look at short-sighted solutions to the problem.

I was the one who mentioned Qassem Soleimani. I follow Haji Qassem very closely. If the more we support the Iranians, the more we fuel the sectarian war, the more we provide a recruiting basis for al-Qaeda. So we must not look at short-term solutions that say let's back Assad because he might be fighting Sunni extremists, let's back Maliki—and I agree with every word you said about Maliki and would add a lot more and not fit for printing—let's just back this guy because he is fighting al-Qaeda. No. That is why we do have to engage in the complexity, painful as it is.

Mr. JONES. Mr. Higgins, Ranking Member Higgins, I just wanted to add two comments to what Dr. Kagan said. No. 1 is: I do think you are right. There is an important Shia-Sunni sectarian component of this. The group we see in Iraq and also in Syria, ISIS, since its origins under Abu Musab al-Zarqawi in western Afghanistan, has been among the most anti-Shia of any of these jihadist organizations. That translated when he went into Iraq before the U.S. invasion and then when he associated himself with al-Qaeda.

He has—this group has been—has committed the most atrocities against Shia. But I would say, more broadly, the largest amounts of violence we have seen in jihadist battlefields has been intra-Sunni. There is intense fighting among Sunni organizations, and this gets me to my second point briefly, which is I think Fred is right, that there is—this is about extremism versus non-extremists. As we have seen these—where these groups have been beaten back in Mali, with French and U.S. participation, in Saudi Arabia in 2003 and other locations, during the Awakening, it has been Sunnis that have pushed them back in areas because their views are too extreme.

I think they will go down and they will go down in part because Sunnis will not accept these extremists, because they do not espouse the views of most Muslims in these areas. Thank you.

Mr. SIMCOX. I think there certainly is battle of sectarian warfare going on and battle for control, but what we have to avoid is the temptation to then just take a step back and say, well, everyone is as bad as each other, we can't do anything about this, and retreat towards isolationism. We have a role to play, and we have a great stake in the outcome. We have a great stake in as best as we can trying to foster democratic movements in that part of the world, because some of these groups that we are worried about and that we are talking about today, their ideology and their ambitions don't stay at their own borders. They ultimately come to affect us in the homeland, so we have to be very active in our engagement in that area.

Mr. HIGGINS. Just a final thought. There is a relatively recent book by Marwan Muasher called "The Second Arab Awakening." In it, you know, he argues that that part of the world is very pluralistic. Unless and until there are, minority rights, these battles will always continue.

So if there is—you know, it is a zero-sum game. So long as there is a zero-sum game, in order for somebody to win, somebody has to lose. Unfortunately, it is not ideal, but it is the reality that civil wars in world history are a part of nation-building. You know, we in our own country had a civil war. About 625,000 people died in the American civil war. At that time, our Nation's population was probably about 38 million people. That is pretty significant.

It just seems that I understand the importance of this. I understand the importance of protecting the homeland. I really do, and I would do anything in my power to support policies to achieve that objective. But the fact of the matter is, everybody has been wrong, Democrats and Republicans, Democratic administration, Republican administrations, because of the complexity of these kinds of issues.

It just seems to me that more military intervention, if it is viewed as supporting the Maliki government in Iraq, despite the fact that he doesn't deserve American support, because he only came to us when he was threatened. He cut a deal with the Iranians to keep him in power. This is just a vicious cycle that will continue, and there is really no game-changing moment unless and until the warring factions make a decision that in order to progress, they have to coexist peacefully.

You know, a lot of people say that, you know, that is impossible, particularly in that part of the world, but, you know, when you look at the situation in Northern Ireland, the Protestants and the Catholics, they had to do one thing before they were accepted to the negotiating table. They had to renounce violence. They had to renounce violence and then they had to participate in an international process to destroy their arms, to confirm that they were disavowing the tradition, both traditions, both sides of violence, then and only then—and it wasn't unilateralism, it was mutuality—they progressed.

The United States and Great Britain played an extraordinary role in that great achievement, albeit still with problems, but that was a major, major achievement. The United States didn't deploy any military troops. We had great leverage.

So I just think that, you know, we are going to be here 5 years from now, because talking about the same things, because this will require at least another generation. Any involvement, for every action, there is a reaction. It seems as though, when there is a reaction, typically it doesn't accrue to the benefit of the United States.

So I will yield back. Thank you.

Mr. KING. Gentleman from Georgia.

Mr. BROUN. I will just add a little more and just associate myself with what my friend from New York, Mr. Higgins, just said. I think very long-term the basic solution is going to be the non-extremist Muslim saying, "We are not going to put up with this anymore world-wide." Somehow we as a Nation need to foster that type of philosophy within the Muslim community.

Part of our heritage, part of our Constitution, part of what we are all about is accepting people of different religious beliefs. I don't think as a Nation we have really understood how important it is to work with the non-extremist Muslim community world-wide to try to help stop this. Again, I think it is intelligence as well as our special ops people who can help foster this.

Can you all expound upon that philosophy that I have that it is going to be the Muslim community itself that just rejects extremism and stops it world-wide, as opposed to us doing what we have been doing, again, has been all about containment?

Mr. KAGAN. I do agree with you that this ends when—or ends for now when the Muslim community does reject this. But this is not a theoretical political ideological discussion that is being had in the Muslim right now. It is a war. This is something that we really can't lose sight of, because you can be an Iraqi and most Iraqis reject the Islamic State ideology. But that doesn't do you any good if the Islamic State are the guys who have got the guns and the gun trucks sitting on every corner going around, rounding up everybody who speaks against them, killing them.

If you don't have an ability to defend yourself against those people, then disagreeing with their ideology is just an extravagant way of committing suicide. We have done this before. With respect to the Ranking Member, not everything we have done has failed and not everything that we have tried has been a mistake.

We did enable the Iraqi Sunni community to turn against al-Qaeda in Iraq in 2007. We did support them, and they did reject them, and they put 100,000 of their own sons into the front line against this organization. Now, Maliki screwed that up, absolutely, right with you on that, sir. But they did turn. What made them turn? One of the things that made them turn was the belief that they would win, that they would fight, they would bleed, they knew that, but when they came to believe that they could win, they were willing to do that. We had to help them believe that they could win.

So what I would say is, no one is advocating a blanket, large-scale military intervention around the world. That is not what we are talking about. Although this committee is not engaged in this, there is a lot of straw man discussion that is going on in town where people are saying, oh, you just want to send hundreds of thousands of troops. I don't know anybody who is advocating doing that.

What I am going to say is that from the standpoint of answering the question: Who is capable of helping moderate Muslims defeat militarily the people who are attempting to impose this ideology upon them by force? That capability does not exist within the Muslim community right now.

Our alternative is going to be, we are either going to help provide that capability to defeat this organization so that what you are describing can occur, which I believe it will, or we can have this protract for a much longer period of time, have many, many, many more people die, including our own, and have this movement spread.

I believe we can affect this. Although I absolutely do understand that every action we take has a consequence and there are going to be unforeseen consequences, we also need to recognize that inaction has consequences and very frequently unforeseen, but in this case very foreseeable consequences.

One of those is, is that if no one takes action to help moderate Muslims defeat the armies of extremists they are now facing, those armies will triumph for quite some time and the situation will get a lot worse.

Mr. BROUN. I agree with you. Again, I think it is our intel community and our SF and special ops military forces that are going to pay a key role in doing just that.

Mr. Chairman, if you will give me one more question, I would appreciate it, because I believe the policies of four administrations—two Republicans and two Democrats now of open borders—and they have—both Bush administrations, the Clinton administration, as well as now the Obama administration—have absolutely refused to secure our borders. To me, that is a National security issue. I think the United States is becoming a safe haven, also, because of administrations.

Again, I think it is going to take intel, boots on the ground, not monitoring every American's emails and phone calls, but having the intelligence community in this country, as well as worldwide, to have that human intelligence is absolutely critical for us to make sure that America is as safe as possible.

So I assume all of you all would agree that we need to secure the borders and we need to do it as quickly as possible. Is my assumption correct? Yes, no, all four of you?

Mr. KAGAN. Yes, I would agree with you. But I think the larger point you are making is also very important, that——

Mr. BROUN. Well, absolutely.

Mr. KAGAN [continuing]. The defense of the borders does not start at the border.

Mr. BROUN. No, in fact, a lot—40 percent of the people here in this country illegally—in fact, all of the ones that perpetrated the 9/11 attack came here legally. They just overstayed their visa. That is also a part of the problem that we have as a Nation. We don't know when people come and go, and we are not following them.

Again, four administrations have been guilty of just saying, come if you want to, and we know—people coming across our Southern Border, I am sure across our Northern Border, as well, that are—the Department of Homeland Security and CBP calls them OTMs, other than Mexicans. We are capturing folks from the Middle East, from Asia, that are coming across our borders.

But who are we not capturing? With this flood of unaccompanied minors that are coming into this country, it is—that our administration has encouraged is exacerbating the problem that we have from entities coming into this country with other than generous reasons towards helping the United States or for economic reasons. I think they are coming here.

So I would appreciate just a written idea from all of you all, too, about—and I am going to ask a question for you to answer about the funding, if you would, please answer that in writing about—again, we see Iran funding Hezbollah, as well as Hamas, both sides, from Sunni, as well as Shia. Iran is a huge part of this issue, and I don't see this administration or the previous administration really dealing with Iran to the strength that we need to.

If you all have any suggestions about doing so, Mr. Chairman, my time is up, unless they want to have a comment.

Mr. KING. Actually, if you could do it in writing, I would appreciate it, because we are running short on time.

So—the gentleman from Florida.

Mr. CLAWSON. A little economic practicality here might be in order. I think that the idea that we are the only arbiter in the Arab world as this religious political civil war plays out bothers me a little bit. Our trade deficit with Arab nations and with oil-exporting nations, it is hundreds of billions of dollars. They should be part of this solution. It is their neighborhood, and it is our money that goes from our consumer to their pocketbooks. Where are the gulf nations?

We have had this conversation today, where that hasn't even come up. We should not be funding this. We are paying them. We are paying for our oil, first of all. I think I am in agreement with the Ranking Member that this is going to be such a complicated thing. It is so difficult, because it is the intersection of Government and religion which makes it a lot different than a lot of civil wars that we have seen. It has been going on for centuries.

I think in the Muslim world, now means 100 years time frame, and America now means a week. Their now is a very long now, isn't it not, gentlemen? So, therefore, I revert back to what I am worried about for us, our allies, and especially Israel, what—assuming we can't solve this program anytime soon, I am worried about the supply chain, coming through Europe or, to your point, Mr. Jones, straight to the United States. It matters not to me all of our intelligence and all of our resources to cut off people that are going to do us and our enemies harm.

I am not saying, Mr. Congressman Broun or Mr. Brookes, that we shouldn't be engaged there—you know, with special forces or anybody else. I am saying I think that is a very difficult situation that won't be solved anytime soon, even if we do pull the right knobs, and in the mean time, let's cut off the supply chain. Any communication to me that we can do to help or that I can do to help, I am all ears.

I yield back.

Mr. KING. I want to thank the witnesses for their testimony. I would just say, in conclusion for myself, this could be a battle and struggle that goes on for decades, centuries, whatever. My concern is the innocent Westerners that are killed in the mean time. As far as whether or not we have had success, the fact is, there has not been a major attack on our mainland since September 11, 2001. To me, that is a success.

It didn't happen just because you waited for it to resolve itself. It is because we did take aggressive action, not always done perfectly, but the fact is, we took action, and I think it is because of that that we are a safer Nation today or at least we have been protected more—since 9/11 than we have before. I think emerging threats could make it more dangerous, but that would even exacerbate itself if we lowered our defenses.

As far as the question of intelligence, I think it is absolutely essential. The gentleman from Georgia and I can have a debate, because I don't believe the NSA is listening to anyone's phone calls or reading anyone's emails, but that is another story for another hearing.

But if we don't fully use our intelligence capabilities and don't maximize our potential, I believe that—while the Sunnis and the Shias and the fragmentation within the Sunnis is being resolved, I don't want Americans killed in the mean time. Mr. Simcox doesn't want Europeans killed, nor do I, and I think that is really what this is about, how we keep enough pressure on to protect us and protect the homeland. I don't think any of us ever wants to go through another 9/11.

So with that, the hearing stands adjourned. I thank the witnesses for their testimony. As the gentleman from Georgia said, any questions that you want to respond to in writing, he is more than willing to take them. Thank you.

[Whereupon, at 11:43 a.m., the subcommittee was adjourned.]

○